For Mom

Each one of us a
Star of light and love,
God loves us as His own!

Constance.

5th May 2007.

Paradise, A Heartbeat Away

A Spiritual Safari in Africa

By Constance van Dongen Eykman

Published by Tiki Books

Paradise, A Heartbeat Away
A Spiritual Safari in Africa,
By Constance van Dongen Eykman
Copyright, 2005 by *Constance van Dongen Eykman*. All rights reserved.
Cover art by Costyn van Dongen Eykman, All rights reserved
Published by Tiki Books

Library and Archives Canada Cataloguing in Publication
Dongen, Constance van, 1940-
    Paradise, a heartbeat away : a spiritual safari in Africa /
by Constance van Dongen Eykman
ISBN 1-897222-04-1
    1. Dongen, Constance van, 1940- 2. Spiritual life.
3. Spiritual
biography--Africa. 4. Africa--Biography. I. Title.
BL73.D65A3 2005   204'.092   C2005-
902929-3

For additional information about quantity discounts, autographed books, co-branded books and special promotions, please contact Tiki Books via our website at www.TikiBooks.com

I dedicate this book to my fellow travelers on the safari of life on this planet.

"I refuse to call anyone an atheist or an unbeliever, for all are Creations of the Lord and repositories of Grace.
In everyone there is a spirit of Love, a rock of Truth. That Love is God, that Truth is God. Divinity is there, in the depth of everyone's Inner Being."

ఊ   ౭

Sri Sathya Sai Baba

Contents

Thank You   vii

Foreward   ix

Preface   xi

A Symphony In Black and White   1

Paradise   3

We Are The Toddlers of The Universe   15

Royal Rooster   29

Mwangi, Little Mwangi   39

Love On Prescription   47

Paradise Lost   63

Paradise Recreated   77

And Then One Day   91

The Streets of Nairobi   103

A Cuckoo on the Equator   111

From Hell to Heaven in Maseno   117

Finale   127

About The Author   129

Thank You

Pieter, my playmate, you pulled me into your story, and then took me away from all I had ever known. All these years you supported and encouraged me in everything I did. You kept me free of worldly duties to learn to listen to my heart, act upon it, and reach my destiny: to be a teacher of the heart.

Costyn, beloved third in the one-ness that we are, your love and joy and inner knowing were, and still are, a source of strength and stability in our adventurous existence. For you both this painting of our life.

Han, my Down's syndrome brother, who died in 1995 with Alzheimer, your life has been the beginning of my asking 'why' from a very early age on. I loved you so deeply that I could never accept life as a coincidence, nor God as someone who allows in one family a daughter with all the possibilities to unfold, and a son with the same gifts and talents, but then blocks him from expressing those in the world.

You from 'the other side of the veil', my ancestral lineage, you formed the genetic stream in which my soul could embed itself in this lifetime. I thank you for being with me in far past, in the present and in future.

Joseph Donders, my priest and friend and 'guru', your prayers supported me when, at times, life seemed to be beyond my strength. Lovingly you followed my mystical unfolding, and with your being and your life wrapped around our beloved Jesus, you are a lighthouse in my search to find a way to be like him. The simplicity, with which you write and tell our Jesus to the world, has formed mine.

Dr. Zulfiquar Jaffery, very dear physician, for many years you have helped me through the pain of my damaged spine with undemanding and respectful patience. Without you, I might have given up and I am so grateful to still be here. Together with you I thank your colleagues who were important in my life and stood model for the ones in this book.

Janet Allen Mwangale, thank you for sharing with me your gift to see and hear where the senses cannot reach. Jesus I 'knew by heart' but with you I learned to know Sathya Sai Baba, and the wisdom, love, compassion and humor of our teacher and guide into the love of God.

We traveled a road of fifteen years. We laughed, we cried and we 'pushed each other's buttons', but the yearning for the God of Love in our hearts was not left unanswered. God's Grace merged us into one being with two pair of eyes—to serve the world in love and gratitude. I love you, my sister Spirit-in-the-Wind.

John Harricharan, you saw in me my stories when I was too tired of the complications of life in Africa to even think of writing them. Thank you for leading me on this path of healing, and then of joy! Your loving guidance has given me the confidence to reveal my inner world to the eyes of the world.

And then there are all who walked the path with me in search of the peace of God. I hold you with me in my soul into all eternity: Mardeleine, sweet mother of 'little Krishna', and Rosy and Kishin Kubchandani, his grandparents; Father Tom McDonnell, Mandy Parkin, Heather Campbell, Patricia Roskens, Bhuvana and Ramanan, Michael Kibinge, Kay Blackwell, Jayman Shukla, Nicola Smyth, Chris and Margarita Hawly, Viju, Raghu, Nina, and Madhu Raghunath, Joost and Elke de la Rive Box, Joan Brinch and Mathias Guepin, Frederique Grootenhuis, Jaleeh Eshani and many others—and you who lived with us for so long: Rose, Gathua, Christopher, David, Leonida and Jacob, Paul and Florence.

And lastly, I thank Anita Bergen, Judy Seton, Pieter and Costyn van Dongen for helping me with editing the manuscript.

Foreword

Reading this book will help the reader to see that our existence is full of mystery. That is why the world deserves our full attention. Any introduction to a more spiritual life insists on that condition. Wendell Berry once wrote: "My most inspiring thought is that this place, if I am to live well in it, deserves a lifetime of the most careful attention."

Any place can yield wonders when we – prayerfully, reverently and respectfully - stay open for the mystery, the spiritual power that is the carrier and substance of all we are interwoven with in our lives. All of us can sharpen our lives by living in the awareness of this certainty, awakening from the illusion of our apparent unrelatedness.

Those paying attention to this spiritual reading of life have sometimes been calling it the 'Kingdom of God'. Others have been giving it other names; but every part of reality will tell its story to those who are curious enough to listen and to see from moment to moment.

The reason that many do not see this 'mysticism' in everything is because to them there does not seem anything special to see in the ordinary. Their actual way of life pushes them to be so busy and distracted, that it threatens to reduce them to superficial surface-surfers of their world without any further depth, meaning, or content.

The world is a frighteningly barren place, if you only see, hear, taste and touch in that frivolous way. No wonder that the public interest in a more profound response to this apparent emptiness is growing by the day.

It is in this context that Constance van Dongen Eykman's book "Paradise, A Heartbeat Away" is like a deep, fresh breath of air, or even better of spirit. In it she tells how in the warp and the woof of her life one golden thread keeps

Flowers and children;
African, American, European, and Indian friends;
A Christian background and an Indian Guru;
Crystals and children;
Sickness and health;
Angels and cosmos;
God and humanity;
Past, present and future;
Paradise and world;
Animals and trees
together in a dynamic way.

Behind all this, or within, she discovered in her adventures a kind of drawing force, an attraction, a transcendent power that reveals itself as Love. Some might call it serendipity, others synchronicity, again others divine providence. And Paul wrote in his letter to the Romans: "We know that by turning everything to their good God cooperates with all those who love." (8:28).

The author discovered also another consequence. By simply and honestly paying attention you find out how to live life and what needs to be done.

Discoveries the author will help others to make in their own lives!

Prof. Dr. J. G. Donders
Former Professor and Chairman of the Department of Philosophy
and Religious Studies, at Nairobi University, Kenya.

Preface

I have good news for you. The world is changing for the better! We are learning to listen to each other's needs. Even though massive obstacles seem to prove the contrary, the understanding is growing that we have not come to this earth only for ourselves but to be part of the whole.

Societies grow towards a democratic emancipation of its members, which allows individuals to grow. At the same time, like the European Union after centuries of wars, nations pull together in order to experiment with a new collectivity.

United Nations, World Health Organization, World Food Program and countless governmental and non-governmental organizations assist individuals and groups to develop within their own countries and in the world at large. The global heart is opening up.

For me, a crash course in opening up was to move away from 'home' in the Netherlands to Africa in 1980. On a continent and among a race that were alien to me, I learned that each encounter with another is an opportunity to open up in us a well of love and respect we did not know we had.

Another part of my course was, for ten years, to be withdrawn from normal life with a physical problem. This created an opportunity to live without the distractions of the outer world and turn inward. My day-to-day consciousness expanded to realities beyond the ones we normally perceive, and made me aware of a deeper truth in all that happens in and around our lives.

The way back to health was the path towards personal inner peace—with all the work it takes to achieve this. It took me into the heart where lies a deep sense of belonging.

Peace on earth only comes as a reflection of inner peace. To expect 'others' to achieve it for us—be it politicians, doctors or Christ in the Second Coming—will happen no more than Jesus fixing it all for us 2000 years ago. We all are part of the process.

Peace is inclusive; it does not leave anyone out. And so is love. All power is ephemeral, except the power of undemanding, selfless love. It connects us with the stars, with people, animals, plant life and the very soil we walk on.

I have my history and you have yours, but the underlying story is the same. We are on safari, a journey to fill an emptiness in our heart, a search for fulfillment, which can only be achieved by connecting with the hearts of others.

Everywhere in the streets, in restaurants, shops, airports, trains, or even while riding a bike, I see people with a mobile phone glued to their ears. Are they yearning for a voice to whisper, "Do you need me? Do you love me? Are you as lonely as I am? Can we do something together?"

We send each other signals, but they are the softest whispers, not always audible while we are on the move. They can be heard in an inner listening that makes us look at a child, tugging at our sleeve, or smile at a stranger in the street whose eye we happen to catch, in answer the unspoken question: "Tell me, am I loved?"

The words channeling, spiritual healing, connecting with minds and hearts in distant parts of the world or even at 'the other side of the veil', indicate different ways of listening, with the inner antennae reaching into worlds beyond the five senses—where the heart can easily go.

I understand God as 'He-She-It', the all-encompassing Consciousness, the love and the truth we are part of and that bind us. For convenience sake, I have used the traditional 'He' to indicate God.

'Paradise A Heartbeat Away' are my stories in which a moment of listening to a silent voice, an urge to do something I had never planned but which seemed to be in harmony with my heart, opened a panorama of happenings, emotions, and healing I had no idea ever existed, neither in the material world nor in the cosmic one. Just as not listening, too, had repercussions beyond anything I ever expected.

Creation has possibilities that go beyond our wildest dreams—or nightmares. The choice is ours more often than we think, in that split second of the 'now'.

A profound and joyful world lies hidden within ours. I invite you to mine.

With all my heart!

Constance van Dongen Eykman

A Symphony in Black and White

"My Africa, my other Africa, so filled with love and laughter! I want to honor you and tell your story to the world. I want to paint your smile, and sing for all your gentle eyes that stir my heart. I witnessed your devotion, and your defenselessness has taught me mine. Your living in the moment, the most precious time we have, showed me the courage to endure. You taught me lessons on the wealth we think we need—and how tough a teacher you could be! You, who wear your heart so close at hand, you brought me peace."

In 1980 the symphony of life took the three of us to Kenya, my husband Pieter, our three-year-old son Costyn and me. The Dutch prelude was over—forever, as I did not know then. The next movements we had to compose on a continent and among a race we did not know, in a capital of a country where everything and everyone were unfamiliar. The symphony changed key, pitch, and tempo. From pianissimo to forte, the melody changed fast from flat to sharp and back. In breathtaking presto to solemn slow lento, themes came together, sometimes clashed, disentangled and flowed in harmony again.

Through the whole, however, weaved the song of rondo, the most beautiful movement of all—the dance in a circle. Here we take each other's hand, black, white and brown, and dance around to the tune of God. Its beautifully interwoven melodies and rhythms are Christian, Moslem, Hindu, Sikh, Baha'i and Buddhist. In Nairobi I learned to love them all.

Life in an entirely different community is looking in the mirror and not always liking what we see: a white person from the rich world, often generous and compassionate indeed, but also impatient, proud, tense, and always in such a hurry that we often do not feel how rude we are to the other's inner culture.

It takes love to see that it is we who are the note of discord and not 'the other'. It takes courage to rewrite parts of the music and learn to play it afresh. And so I gave my inner orchestra to the trusted hands of two renowned conductors: Jesus, and the Indian spiritual leader of mankind Sathya Sai Baba, who both show us God and invite us to be like him.

Withdrawn from active life after an operation on my back that had gone wrong, I learned my new score. And my violin now plays my stories for you of how God walks the earth with us, deep in our hearts where we know love.

Paradise

How God must have enjoyed creating Mother Earth! He colored her with all the sparkling greens he had on his palette and covered her with jewels of blue and turquoise water, deep brown soil, and strong black rocks. To dress her in glorious blue, in one great sweep he painted the sky, and to make her skirt forever flow in the wind, he experimented with his breath. When he blew out through the nose, the wind became cold; hot and humid when he opened wide his mouth, and with pursed lips, he made the wind whistle. Picture him drawing the knobby old trees on her dress, and delicately painting the wings of the butterflies at the border of her sleeves! For every flower he mixed the scent just right, and he wrapped her in the delicate fragrances of flowers, plants, and the soil they grow in, moisturized by the rain.

He gave her animals to play with on the ground, and above the ground the birds, for her to rejoice in their delightful little songs that on a sunny Sunday had welled up in him to sparkle from their throats. All creatures were gentle and peaceful because God gave them the foliage of the plants for food, as the Bible says.

Deep inside the earth, he hid the most splendid minerals, in the waters reflected by the shimmering fish, glowing in the color of the flowers on the earth's surface, and scintillating in the plumage of the birds in the sky.

Then he created humans to walk her surface. As the bearers of his Mind and Heart, these children of him and her were the bridge between heaven and earth.

A little while later he created this old farmhouse in the heart of Africa, perched on the ridge of a steep hill. At the bottom of either side of the hill, small streams murmured down over the rocks in little waterfalls. Like humans who express their extremes of passion and peace, they took on a different face, however, during the seasonal heavy rains. Then they changed into roaring rivers with thundering waterfalls, only to calm down again a couple of hours after the rain had stopped.

In ancient cultures, mountain peaks are often considered to be the home of God or Gods, and hilltops are places of worship. The house stood on a site where the reverence of people who had worshipped since times immemorial still radiated in the light. Deep wisdom from Mother Earth whispered in the immense trees that burst out in delicate, fragrant bloom once a year and made them sing in the humming of the beetles and the bees. When, by the grace of their work, an abundance of small fruits followed the bloom, the colors returned with the birds that came to feast—purple, magenta, bronze green, sunshine yellow, and white.

God gave this place to an Adam and Eve and their child who loved and respected its sanctity and filled it with people from the ancient race. To celebrate their gift, they covered the earth with flowers and completed paradise with animals—lots of them.

We had to move from the house we were living in, and Pieter and I were looking for a new place. We found it on a rainy Sunday afternoon, this old coffee estate house on eleven neglected acres in the outskirts of Nairobi.

Some of the first British settlers, who arrived in Kenya around 1900, had built their initial shelter in the same way as the Africans who assisted them: round huts constructed with wattle and daub and covered with grass-thatched roofs. Most built a 'proper' square house later on, but a few people replaced the mud walls of the rondavels with stones and roofed it with iron sheets. A few of those original structures still exist and this house was one of them.

It was virtually a ruin. The building stones were cut from the solid volcanic rock that had been quarried farther downhill, but no one had bothered to make a foundation in the deep red soil it stood on, and it was only just holding up.

The powerful roots of the trees invited themselves, unhampered, inside the house. They broke up the cement floors, so that the doors scraped over the cracks and could not close. They fractured the walls, which here and there were so badly broken that we could freely look outside. The windows hung on broken hinges. Goats walked through what looked like the sitting room and a chicken perched on a wheel rim that was lying in front of the fireplace. The smoke of a smoldering heap of old leather poisoned the air outside.

The main house consisted of six rondavels, connected by mysterious narrow corridors, some dark, and some with windows.

Behind the kitchen was a guesthouse. It had the cutest little double-storied tower that was crowned with a peaked iron roof and weather vane.

The kitchen itself was small, dark, and shabby. It was all of fifty square feet, with one tiny window high up in the wall. The old sink was the last resting place of two big dried fish. Everything was filthy.

For two years, twenty basket weavers had lived and worked in the house, and the smoldering leather outside was the leftover material for the handles of the kiondo's, these very popular shopping bags. Later on, we learned from the owner that their employer had never paid him the rent, and the workers probably had hardly ever received their wages, either. Smashed windows and holes poked in the ceilings were witness to drunken destruction and probably anger, as well.

The garden surrounding the house, wild and overgrown, had surrendered to ungainly weeds. An immense bamboo bush worked hard to gobble up the dining room.

Next to the house was a borehole. It was functioning, but the water storage tanks on the roof of one of the outbuildings were full of holes. The water poured out as fast as it came in and all the taps were dry. From the doorway of a dilapidated room underneath the tanks, a melancholy goat stared at us with a questioning look in his eyes.

The atmosphere inside the house was gloomy and dark. There were many windows, but they were small and low. From above, they were half covered by the edges of the overhanging iron roofs, and the garden struggled enter inside from below. The roofs were obviously leaking, for in some of the rooms the ceilings sagged down so low in the center that we could hardly walk upright.

The conical roofs were a marvel. They were made of iron sheets, fixed with rusty nails on a patchwork of twigs and branches that had been woven together in any old way. They looked like pointed hats, put askance on a bunch of gnomes gathered in a meeting, and the soft reddish brown of the flaking paint made the whole structure merge with the color of the soil. It was magic. On top of the hill, as a cluster of organically grown mushrooms, the place blended in with nature around it. And it radiated with a soft inner light.

When we walked out of the gate again, Pieter and I looked into each other's eyes and exchanged a flash of intense excitement. We had found the material of fairy tales!

We found out that the present owner was a Kikuyu— the tribe, which lives in the area stretching from Nairobi to Mount Kenya—and Pieter tracked him down in his little shop downtown. When he asked him if we could rent the place, the man was dumbfounded. Then slowly the wheels of his mind began to turn,

"Oh well, if these crazy white people want the hovel and are even prepared to pay for it, I'd better jump at the chance!"

Pieter had just started his own groundwater-consulting firm, and he was happy when they could agree on a very low rent, fixed for five years. The landlord was willing to do the basic repairs and renovations, but we would have to pay ourselves for luxuries like elevating the ceilings and extending the kitchen. Compared to us, the Kikuyu are often small in stature, and he laughed at us: the ceilings were just fine and the kitchen was big enough.

And anyway, since there was plenty of firewood, it was much cheaper for 'Mama' to cook outside—which I did for some time, by the way—the dog food, that is.

Months of renovation followed. I spent most of my days supervising the work, since the criteria of the contractor often differed somewhat from ours. When, for instance, the masons, who were also much smaller than I, cut a window in the new wall of the kitchen extension, they placed it so low that I had to bend over to be able to look outside. Of course they objected that it was 'not possible' to change it, when I asked them to, but after some convincing they took it out again and placed it higher up in the wall, among lots of laughter at our difference in size.

One day I came in and a fundi—someone who makes or repairs things—had just finished sawing nice big holes right in the center of every single new ceiling we had to pay for ourselves. The reason? One needed access to the electricity wiring under the roof, didn't one? He was flabbergasted when I nearly exploded with anger.

The work was by no means finished by the time we had to leave our other house. For three more months, the workers were still all over the place. Electricians completed the wiring; masons, carpenters, painters and unskilled laborers were finishing walls, doors, and windows, and repainting the roofs. Some more were outside, digging in pipes and a septic tank. At times the only place left for me to hide was the bathroom, until someone knocked at the door to connect or disconnect something or other, but at least we were in.

Christmas came, and they all had left. From floors to roofs the house was now renovated. We were happy and they had all been so proud. Never before had they cemented round walls so smoothly; never had they been challenged to elevate the ceiling of a rondavel with a conical roof. Their patchwork of soft board, cut in the most interesting geometrical shapes, over the years never ceased to endear us.

Even in all the chaos, we had felt embraced by the round walls of the house. The deepest meaning of our collective effort seemed to have been to cleanse the ancient holy site of unhappy memories and negative energies it had gathered over the years of its long life. The house felt reborn and ready for a new consciousness to be brought in.

It was situated on the municipal boundary of Nairobi, close to a village that even the local people called a 'thieves' den'. The majority of the Kenyans live in desperate poverty and, more and more robbery, often violent, is the last way out of despair for the destitute. We needed watchmen to protect us at night, and we wanted two Samburu, our favorite people for this job.

The Samburu, tribal cousins to the Maasai, live just above the equator, where the foothills of Mount Kenya merge into the northern desert. They are a proud warrior race of cattle-owning pastoralists, and their social organization is based on raising livestock.

Boys are circumcised in their early teens in a group ritual that is attended by the entire village. Once they have gone through this rather rough and painful operation without flinching—which would dishonor their families—they are no longer considered to be a child. They join the group of other young men who have undergone circumcision before them, and they are the warriors, the Moran. It is their task to protect the clan and its cows, sheep, goats, and camels against enemies and wild animals. They live away from the villages until their late twenties, when, with great ceremony, they are accepted as junior elders of the clan. They are also allowed to marry, then.

One of the admission requirements is to catch and kill a lion, armed with nothing but a short knife and a spear. With expressive body gestures and rolling eyes, the Moran told us how this is done. With five or six men they surround a lion. One of the group challenges it until it is enraged, and when the lion attacks, the other Moran jump at it and with their bare hands pull the legs from under the animal. Once it is down, the leader of the group cuts its throat with his knife. Of course they usually sustain quite some wounds in this daring event.

So, any thief who values his life knows better than to try and rob a place guarded by Samburu. We asked around, and soon watchmen of the neighbors, who were of the same tribe, came to introduce two of their friends. Pieter greeted them and asked the usual polite questions:

"What is your name? Where do you come from, and how was the safari (travel)?"

They looked him in the eyes with a mixture of shyness and their habitual pride. Their English was just enough to make us understand them.

"We are from Maralal (about 350 kilometers north of Nairobi)."

"How long did it take you to get here?"

"Only three days!" was the proud answer.

"You did not come by bus?"

"We came 'footing'. We walked during the night and we slept only four hours in the afternoon when it was too hot to go on." They looked as if we could trust them with our lives, and Pieter hired them.

Our Moran were proud young men—fierce, tall, and sinewy. They walked with the long stride of those who have walked the savanna plains forever, the magnificent gait with which they had walked to Nairobi in three days and nights. They wore their traditional hairstyle: long, plaited in thin, tight braids, and colored with red ochre. They usually kept it tucked away in a large, multicolored, knitted cap.

They lived in small rooms on our compound. After a cold night outside, we could see them sit in the morning sun for hours, warming up and braiding each other's hair. Once a year, they went home on leave and if one returned with his long hair cut off, we knew he had gone through the final initiation ceremonies and was now a junior elder, and probably had married as well.

When a celebration was called for, they dressed up to the nines. They draped a red cloth around their body, which left legs and one shoulder bare and put sandals, cut from car tires, on their feet. They decorated cheeks and torso with symbols in red-brown mud, ornamented their neck and wrists with spectacular bead necklaces and bracelets, and hung pendants in their elongated earlobes. They looked splendid, strong and ancient.

At times they danced. Both Maasai and Samburu have a way of dancing, which is completely different from all other Kenyan styles. They hold their bodies very erect and, their arms stretched along their sides, with straight legs they jump high up in the air. The others encourage them with clapping, and sing a rhythmic, "Ooah! Ooah! Ooah!"

Moses was a friendly, cheerful young Samburu. He was a musician. In one end of a gray PVC pipe, half an inch wide and about thirty inches long, he had made two small holes. Somehow he adjusted his mouth to the other end and artfully blew in it. This was his flute.

For hours on end, in the star-studded tropical night he sent up monotonous melodies in a never-ending variety of rhythms. They blended in with the sounds of the crickets and the frogs, the nightjars, the owls, and the screams of the bush babies playing in the trees. Sometimes we asked him to play under the window of our child, to send him off to sleep, weaving Africa into his being.

It was a late Saturday afternoon. The members of the staff who lived on the compound had left to socialize or to go to church, and Pieter and Costyn, too, had gone out. I was unwell and I had stayed behind. Around six o'clock Moses came on duty and saw me resting on a bed in front of a window. He lifted his hand in greeting in response to mine, and walked to the guardhouse at the gate to take his chair. But instead of putting it next to the gate, his usual spot, he carried it under the magnificent wild fig tree in front of my window and sat down where I could see him. He took out his flute and, without saying a word, began to play.

He knew how I loved it, and at first he played for me. But as the light changed into sunset, then dusk, then night, and the stars appeared in the sky, he played for himself. Evermore he seemed to sink deeper within his own being until there was nothing but the sound of his flute, and I sensed how he was back in the endless plains of the country of his youth, alone with the stars, God, and his own heart.

In those hours, his love for Mama—as they called me— blended with my love for Moses in the sound of a piece of gray PVC pipe. Oh, Africa, there is no heart like yours on this planet!

In the back of the garden we had a workshop for the cars that constantly had to travel to the remotest areas of the country to do groundwater investigations. We could only afford cars past the age of six to ten years old, so there was always plenty of work for the two mechanics Pieter employed. Their work fascinated Moses.

All morning, he hung about the workshop while he was supposed to sleep after his night's work, and slept during the night when he had to guard us. Our warnings not to neglect his job had no effect, and so in the end we decided to give him what he wanted most. The head mechanic was happy to take him on and he became an eager and intelligent student.

This career, however, came to a very unfortunate end. Late one afternoon, he and David, one of the gardeners, got into an argument while they were clearing away their tools to go home. David, who was from another tribe and not trained to fight, gave Moses a shove. This triggered Moses' reflexes of years of training in fighting for his life if need be, and in an instinctive reaction, he hit David on the head with the wrench he happened to have in his hand. I knew something serious was the matter when I was called from the meditation room in the small tower, where no one ever disturbed me. I found David lying on the ground, half unconscious and bleeding. Clearly, there was no time to sort out the confused account of the others and I asked one of the mechanics to get the camper van out to take him to the nearest hospital. The men lifted him in the car, laid him on the bed we had pulled out, and a few minutes later we were on our way. Thinking of his family who depended on him, the poor man was frantic; but fortunately, a scan of his head showed that he needed no more than a few stitches and a painkiller. When we came back home, Moses had fled.

We had no idea where he had gone, and however much we inquired with his colleagues all over the neighborhood, none of them 'knew anything'. We thought we would never see him again Two months later, however, he suddenly turned up, accompanied by a senior elder of his clan. In his distress he had gone back home, where he trusted the council of elders to help him solve his predicament. They had apparently decided that one of them should escort him to Nairobi and, in the old traditional way, they came to ask for an official meeting—a baraza—with David to apologize and ask for his forgiveness. After long hours of talk, this was graciously granted.

And then, sweet, absurd boy, Moses came to me to ask for money to pay amends for the suffering of the gardener! I knew his honor was only half saved as long as this had not been done, but we had paid the hospital expenses and hired an extra help while the gardener could not work, and this truly was too much. I am afraid I refused.

He asked to be taken back to the job and his education, but for obvious reasons this was not possible.

"Mama, David has already forgiven me," he pleaded with us.

"Bwana (sir), I will never do it again, I promise!"

We had to explain to him that he was dangerous in a mechanic workshop when the warrior rose up in him. This time he—and we—had been lucky, but with all the heavy workshop tools at hand, things might turn out differently the next time. We could not take that risk. Of course we offered him his old job back, but being a night watchman had become a mindless occupation to him, and so we had to let him go. We were all sad and we missed him for a long time.

The only reason why we could live in this big, ramshackle house with five acres of garden to maintain was because labor is cheap in poor countries. This sounds like exploitation, but the reality is that it is rather selfish not to employ people. The state does not take care of anyone poor, old, sick or starving.* Without work, people have no money to live on, or feed and educate their children, nor do they have access to healthcare. Even though the salaries are low by western standards, one person with a decently paid job can take care of not only his or her own family, but also parents and grandparents, as well as the education of siblings.

---

* The new government, which came into power in early 2003, has introduced free education at the primary level, and is now in the process of re-introducing free health care for the poor.

Our little crowd consisted of two housekeepers, two gardeners and two night watchmen. There was a separate group of houses in the backyard in which each had a room. It was a fascinating little village—exemplary in a country where, at times, tribal strife still flares up. Here, the different tribes peacefully lived together: Luo, Kikuyu, Samburu, Wakamba, Abaluya and Borana. Some stayed with us for years, others came and went.

At times, there were delightful children. One and a half year old Lekule was the child of our Borana watchman and his Rendille wife Rukia, who worked for me in the house.

Lekule and I loved to walk through the garden together in the evening. We admired the flowers and their colors, from the tiny ones in the grass to the sunflowers that grew higher than the house. Sometimes I picked a flower he liked to give to his Mummy and make her happy.

Hand in hand, we discussed life.

"Mama look, Mpussy!'

"Yes darling. Pussy is called Chui."

"Mpussy mbaya (bad)?"

"No, pussy is very sweet. Come, stroke her."

And as he patted the cat rather roughly on the head, I admonished: "Gently, look, very gently."

Our final destination was the chicken pen with the last snack of the day for the chickens. They knew we were coming and they had already gathered inside the pen after their afternoon freedom. Taking a few grains of maize in his chubby little hand, Lekule called them,

"Chickooni! Chickooni! Come, eat up!" Thrilled that they heeded his call, he threw the grains all of a few inches away from his feet, the way toddlers do, but then got a bit scared when all these big, well-fed hens came rushing towards him.

The chickens also had their share of the farm work. They assisted us in making compost. In the corner of their pen under a jacaranda tree, we always kept a heap of organic matter that had already been decaying in the compost pit for a considerable time. We kept them locked in till around midday, and then gave them food. This way, they hungrily scratched and pecked the heap for insects to eat all morning, and in the meantime mixed in their droppings to make nice, strong manure. After they had been fed, we let them free to roam. I loved their contented chuckle around the house—the sound of peace.

In the center of the complex of rondavels stood two magnificent, tall tulip trees—a variety of the Bignoniaceae—and a mulberry tree. Here we created a beautiful, little inner garden. We laid a circular terrace around the mulberry tree; we made half round flowerbeds, and dug a round fishpond, all in harmony with the shape of the rooms.

Within a year's time, the tulip trees with their red flowers stood watch over flowering shrubs and the red and yellow cannas lilies we had planted. Sweet smelling jasmine climbed the walls of the dining room and a cascade of purple petrea eventually covered half a roof. In the fishpond, where goldfish lazily swam around, papyrus waved over the water and the water lilies. A fountain made the sunlight sparkle in rainbow colors, and the tinkling of the water had a cooling effect when it was hot. A stone frog in the center seemed to call in his friends in the evening: the roaring bullfrogs and the tree frogs with their shrill whistle.

Around a shrub that flowered all through the year, we constructed a big aviary for Kasuku, the parrot. He loved to suck the honey from its yellow flowers and, with his large grey beak, he delicately picked the peas from the seedpods. As the cage was surrounded by kitchen, guestroom, dining room, and sitting room, it was the perfect spot for the bird to participate in the comings and goings of people and animals.

Kasuku was an African Grey, the greatest imitator among all birds. He barked like the dogs, screamed like a couple of fighting cats, and imitated the car horns. He crowed like the rooster and screeched as the kite birds that circled high in the sky. He also ordered the dogs around:

"Kito, out! Jorra, stop it! Tufe, come here!"

Or cajoling: "Chui, puss, puss, puss!"

It was fun to tell people that he could imitate even the goldfish. Their mouths hanging open in amazement, this observation made them look like fish themselves. And it was true! He imitated to perfection the spluttering sound that the fish made when they snapped up the food pellets floating on the surface of the water.

He even murmured the sounds of the local languages the people spoke at the kitchen door, but most perfectly of all he imitated me. My voice is high and light and easy for the bird to reproduce. When I called them, the gardeners or the mechanics did not come from the back of the compound any longer. His loud, "Gathua, Njoroge, Mainaaaa-h!" in my voice, had made them come running in vain too often.

Love expands, and a steady stream of stray dogs and abandoned kittens gradually joined the animals we had brought. Among my happiest memories are the stunned laughter of Pieter and Costyn, or the wise head-shaking of the staff whenever I came home with yet another starving, scrawny dog that I could not leave to die in the streets, or the cutest kitten, which I had found in a cage in the waiting room of the vet.

And a never-ending stream of people...

Pieter had his office in the guestroom behind the kitchen, and all day long colleagues and clients went in and out.

Visitors from many races and religions came for us and for the people who lived on the compound with us. Houseguests stayed from a few days up to half a year in the guestroom we had constructed from the rubble room where the goat had sadly welcomed us.

It was hard work. It was never free of the struggles that are inherent to life on earth.

But if paradise is anything like it, I can't wait.

We are the Toddlers of the Universe

"We are big
And God is small,
I love you, Jesus!"

Little Krishna sang in the full force of his three-year-old voice and his age-old heart.

Everything in me began to dance.

"Listen to him," I exclaimed. "This is so precious!"

His mother's face lit up with a proud little smile.

"Oh please," I begged her, "don't you ever correct him."

Her eyes became round with surprise.

"He knows. He knows more than his religion teachers. This child knows that in truth God is so small that he can live in his very own heart!"

When we were born, we came straight from God and we probably knew him in the same way as Krishna, this child of Christian-Hindu parentage who was singing his truth outside in the garden. As a spiritual being, we had entered the body of a baby, innocent, vulnerable, and defenseless, but as our mind woke up to the world, we gradually lost our intuitive contact with our Source: God, Omnipresent Consciousness, all-encompassing Love. We forgot our origin as Spirit.

One of the ways of dealing with the ensuing unhappiness was—and for many still is—to project its cause on God. To believe that this is his will because we have done wrong in his eyes, even though at times we do not know what the wrong is, and that he needs to be placated before he may allow us to be happy again.

The first Bible Book 'Genesis' tells the story of creation and the consequent 'fall' from paradise. God had forbidden his first created humans, Adam and Eve, to eat the fruit from the Tree of Knowledge of good and evil. When they disobeyed him, they committed what is called the 'original sin': they fell out of love and into fear and reckoned that they were no longer worthy of God's love. The story symbolizes this notion, so deeply etched in many of us, that we need to earn God's love, often through suffering and sacrifice. That it is God's nature to burden us with forever more 'tests' before he can judge us worthy of his love again. And by the way, why do we usually consider tests unpleasant, instead of challenges to our strength? We are afraid that we will fail the demands of whoever is going to mark us. We feel that we are not good enough, and we are convinced that God judges us all unworthy, us, his own beloved creation.

We yearn to return to our original state. We long to feel innocent and to be seen guiltless. We want to love and be loved as we were as children, but to love is being vulnerable and this frightens us so. And how dare we believe that someone loves us, or needs our love—least of all God?

God never willed this. See what happens when we 'fall in love'! We look at the world with the eyes of our heart and all of a sudden, it turns upside down. It gets a shine and paradise appears as it was meant to be. God created us to be permanently in love: with the planet, the minerals, the plants and the animals, with each other and ourselves and, above all, with him as he is with us.

Yes, not only as a parent with his adorable toddler but also as one adult with the other, God is in love with us. He delights in us. He thinks of us day and night. He cannot keep his eyes off us. He just sits and looks, and thinks how perfectly beautiful we are, even if we do not like what we see in the mirror. And there is this delighted gleam in his eyes when we are doing things that make us happy.

He tries to calm us down when we are upset, but if we do not hear anything he says, he calls a few angels to fold their wings around us. When we are scared or sad, he holds us in his embrace and offers us a shoulder to cry on. He laughs about the same things as we do, and nothing makes him happier than if we share everything with him. When we talk to him all day long. When we do not only go to him when we need him, but tell him all the funny, moving, interesting things we see throughout the day. When we sing, laugh, and dance with him, our divine Lover! And he is in bliss when our heart overflows with love and we rush into his arms.

God is love and so are we. God's love is unconditional, and so will ours be once we have surrendered our mind to love instead of fear; when we trust ourselves to be good, as well as the world around us; when finally we dare to allow our mind to be the tool of our heart—as it was created to be. And it is our life's journey to rediscover God, the Source of our innate happiness and love, our trust and vulnerability, our divine innocence.

It is so easy to know God. Little Krishna does!

His small God fills his heart and makes the whole world his home, a place in which he can tumble around in a bubble of joy. People are wonderful too! They exist to be smiled at and to be joked with, to be made to forget that life is so serious and, above all, to be reminded of how it feels to have a heart.

"Unless you become as one of these," Jesus said, pulling a child onto his lap, "you will not enter the Kingdom of Heaven."

We do not have to earn the love of God; it has been ours from the beginning. Does a baby have to earn the love of its mother, or does a toddler have to work hard to deserve the love of daddy? Does the toddler have to atone for falling off the chair when daddy told him not to climb on it? Does his father send him out into the world—as God supposedly did with Adam and Eve—to go through endless painful trials and tribulations, in order to earn the right to be allowed in again when he wants to come home? Little Krishna's God is not like that.

We are the toddlers of the universe. Our Mother Earth supports our feet, nourishes us with her substance, and loves us so much that she receives us back in her womb when we return our life to the Father.

Our Father God is always present, watching our every step. He never goes away to work. We are his work. And when we fall, he picks us up, even though at times we scream so loud with fury and despair that we are not aware that he is holding us.

Our Mother Earth gently nudges us to be careful not to hurt ourselves when we experiment with her matter and her laws.

"If you climb on that chair, you may fall off and hurt yourself."

If we jump down in the right way, we have learned something about matching our size and faculties with the laws of gravity. But, oh boy, if we fall and hurt ourselves, we cry! Then we are the victims of gravity, "The chair did this to me!" The most temperamental among us may kick the chair in anger and hurt ourselves even more. We may decide never to come near a chair again. Or we climb straight back on. Or we rush to Mother and let her kiss the pain away, which is what she loves doing most.

Mother Earth is always there to comfort us, her solace is her beauty and abundance, her clear, crisp winter sky, or the rain that is so needed. She blows us a kiss in a strong wind when we need to cool off, or a gentle one in a soft caress if we call for a soothing touch.

Parents watch their little ones grow, experiment, make mistakes and bear the consequences, and continue to explore and grow. Our earthly father teaches us God's harmony, expressed in the rules of living in society and handling the material world. We go to mother when we are sad and confused because we do not understand why people treat each other the way they do and make every one around unhappy. And when we grow up to experiment with joy and pain on our own, step by step our parents withdraw, but their love for us remains unchanged.

Toddlers are headstrong. In their passion to discover the world, they have such an overwhelming urge to experiment that they often do not listen to advice. They make mistakes and hurt themselves. Does true love punish them by hurting them some more or would it say,

"This was your lesson dear; you wanted to find out for yourself. Now you know."

God gave us a free will to experiment with his creation but, contrary to what Adam and Eve believed according to the story, he does not punish us when we make the wrong choices. Our fear does. Adam and Eve went into hiding after they had eaten the forbidden fruit, but they could have chosen to rush back to God instead and tell him what they had done. They could have told him that their heart was heavy and that they were so sorry, and God would have wrapped them in his loving embrace, which is what he loves doing most!

Mummy and Daddy can never stay cross at a naughty child. When they look in its little face, they see their love for each other, which brought this child to earth. In it, they recognize their own innocence. And this is what God sees in us.

As a mother and father love a baby they brought into the world to celebrate life and their love for each other, so God loves us.

God is love and so are we. We all carry the love of God within us and we know it.

He is the glow of undemanding love that flows from our heart to each other and our child.

What makes us shine when she looks at us, and what do we recognize in his eyes? Love.

What do we feel when we do not fear? Love.

And that is God. There is no love but God's, and all the love we ever experience is his.

He is the peace in our heart or the peace we remember and are yearning for. He is the gratitude in our mind and heart that helps us to forgive and love instead of hate. He is the laughter that bubbles up in us when, for a moment, we forget the past and the future and our baby-joy returns.

It is so easy to love God. Ask little Krishna. Ask the birds in the trees. They don't have their shopping list with worries ready the moment they wake up! As soon as dawn breaks here on the equator, the whole chorus of them bursts out in song. Ten minutes long, they worship. They celebrate the new day. They fill the sky with sound until the air itself seems to vibrate, and only then do they go about their business of finding food.

My God is big and so is yours.

He is the sun and the moon and the stars in the sky and the whole wide world. He is the song of the thrush in spring and early summer and your own voice in the shower that you do not want anyone to hear because you think you cannot sing.

He is the sweet scent of the summer flowers and the appetizing smell of the simple onion frying in your kitchen.

He is the rap singer and his voice, his rhythm, and his words and he is the awesome technique that allows the opera singer to perform the near impossible with her voice. He is the Queen of the Night as Mozart brought her to earth in the grand aria of the Magic Flute.

He is you and I in church and temple, in mosque or prayer room in our moments of exaltation. He is you and I, grumbling or whistling while sweeping the floor. He is the action in us. He is I, sitting behind the computer to write this book, and you who pick it up and read it at this time.

God created us after his own image, the Bible book says. God, Omnipresent Consciousness, once stirred the stillness of his Mind into a thought,

"Let me know and share my Self as love!"

His idea evolved into an image, and this image he bestowed with the Song of his love: 'Om, Aum, Amen: I AM!'

As mist condenses into a drop of water, this sacred, sound-filled Image then descended into ever-denser energy until the Word 'I Am' became the living human, a form on earth at one with Spirit.

We are a Thought of God, expressed in sound and form, as John sings in his Gospel:

"In the beginning was the Word:
the Word was with God
and the Word was God.
He was with God in the beginning.
Through him all things came into being,
and not one thing came into being

except through him." *

I asked him, "Lord of my heart, when you created the mourning dove with its soft sad sound, did you know the grief your children would come to?"

He answered me,

"Let me wipe away your tears

---

* Quoted from the New Jerusalem Bible

dearly beloved,
the joy of my heart
created you.

I give you my Self, sweet child,
I give you each other
and all of creation.
I sing my song for you
  in the morning,
  midday holds you
  in my warmth,
  and in the evening
I offer you peace.
When you sleep at night
I softly call you unto me,
you, my omnipresent joy on earth,
created from my heart."

God is in every single one of us, created from his mind
and heart. We are his love walking on earth. A mere dream our
separation from God's loving heart, a nightmare of confusion, grief
and fear, in reality we are his Self forever. We are his thought,
which encompasses all form and never leaves it. At one with him,
into eternity we live in him with all created for there is nowhere
else to be. Each one of us a star of light and love, unchangeable in
the eternal sky, God knows and loves us as himself. We are very
holy!

In his creation, God paints himself. And in creating an
earthly work of art, we reflect the way the Source of Being feels
inspired to express and share and know himself, and feels
enriched by the results.

From the stillness of my being beyond my mind, a
painting wells up in me. A longing to share my inner song stirs me
into action and, as my creative joy flows out in paint on canvas, I
make it visible in matter.

Shades of paint become a symphony of colors and shapes
come into being as my mind envisaged them. And once my work is
finished, I know myself as the excitement that the colors and the
infinite possibilities of blending them have caused in me. I know
and love myself as the joy inspired by its creation, and in the
beauty of the accomplished expression of my being, my inner
radiance is mirrored back to me.

When visitors come to my studio and go round in wonder,
taken up in the magic that covers the walls, they experience
themselves and me in a deeper way. They reveal to me the Source

we share and, as I become aware of it in others, I learn to know God, myself, and the others: we are God's indwelling glory!

And so God knows himself as love and joy and beauty when we live in his creation in wonder and delight. We are God's mirror—as God is ours.

God does not keep himself to himself. He created the heavens and the earth with all living creatures on it, and when he saw that it was good, he gave it in the care of man and woman. In the same way, I do not paint to keep my paintings to myself. It is my function to share them, as it is theirs to be shared.

Once a painting is finished, it can begin a life away from me. But even if I sell it and it leaves me, I can never truly lose it. It's image lives on in my consciousness as a memory.

As in water ripple touches ripple, the effect of my creation moves outward. If it hangs in someone's sitting room, it may enter the consciousness of visitors as well and, if it touches them, it becomes part of their mind and heart, too. They take it home in their memory and, once in a while, its recollection may briefly bring back the same emotion as at first sight. Imagine how a thought of the painting's harmony and colors brings a smile to someone's face in the middle of a busy day at work; how a colleague catches it and, lifted out of an unhappy mood, goes on then with her day, changed, to warm some others with her smile. My work of art becomes a bridge to others; we all share something now. Connected in the Source, which is the origin of the painting as well as of the feelings it evokes, we have become a family.

The feelings it awakens in others enrich me as they flow back into my heart, and my painting has become Spirit once more, the source of a new expression.

God as Source is infinite, as is my source of inspiration. It never fails me. Embedded in my physical being, though, it seems subjected to restrictions of time and space and physical needs. I can manifest my inspiration only as time allows me. I cannot paint the full twenty-four hours between one sunrise and the next. I have to perform acts, inherent to life in matter and society. My body needs to eat and sleep. I have to shop for food, take the car to the garage, and go and pay the electricity bill at the other end of town. I cannot live alone. I need time with other people. I need the exchange of feelings and experiences. I need the brother-sisterhood of wo-man.

All limitation, however, is illusion. Nothing can affect the source in me. Not for a single moment has its flow been limited or interrupted by any of those activities in which I seemed to be away from it. Day or night, as soon as I am quiet and turn within, visions and ideas present themselves in a never-ending stream.

In the same way, God's love for us, his paintings, is neither limited, nor affected by what we think, believe, or do. It remains untouched—albeit maybe tinged with a little passing sadness if, as may happen to a painting after many years, we put our memory of Spirit in the darkest corner of the house, in theattic, or in the very trash. His and our holiness are unaffected, for we are the unique creation of his mind and heart.

Even though the canvas of the finished painting is concealed, as its foundation it is forever present. The canvas of God's painting is love and our whole life is a yearning for that love.

Switch on the radio and it will not take more than a few seconds to find some singer crooning about love.

A memory stirs even in its poorest substitutes. In the degradation of love that is the sex industry, from advertising to the ignoble porno on late-night TV, sounds a despairing cry for love. Child abuse expresses the utter anguish of those who feel they have forever lost the canvas–white of their innocence, to the extent that they have to hurt it and humiliate it to the ground in order to make it as vile as they feel themselves to be— so that they will never have to look it in the eye again. As desperate a cry for love as can be heard!

In corrupt leaders of nations and in the present day financial downfall of big corporate institutions, theft surfaces in evidence of an insatiable greed. Greed is fear, and fear is the base of all deceit. Fear, that one bad day there will be not enough and we will perish in want, because neither heaven nor earth nor any human being loves us.

Urged on by longing, by an undefined feeling of lack that we translate in many ways, in all the corners of the earth we search for the foundation of the painting of our life. We hope to find it elsewhere, so we travel the globe to its farthest ends. Society has to be better, other, and different to suit our inner need. We expect 'others' and 'outside' to provide us with the fullness we believe we lack. Relentlessly we try to change everyone around us, individuals and groups, and even those we love.

We are on a quest for the love we do not feel for ourselves, an emptiness, which others have to fill because we have failed, still fail, and always will fail. The world and other people have to heal us from our sense of failure and of loss, but they cannot succeed because we are insatiable in our belief in lack and we never trust whatever love and comfort they have to offer us. In mistrust then we cannot see the world but forever failing us, and ceaselessly we put the pressure in a higher gear to make it yield what we believe we need.

We try to change all and everything, until our heart fails, our immune system breaks down, and our society and our whole world falls apart. We have lived in exile from the love of God in our heart for so long, that now our health, our wealth and, above all, our beliefs are in shambles.

We feel powerless rejects of life, refugees on the bare earth. With no more outer world to change, we are thrown back upon ourselves. We stand with empty hands and we look around at nothingness.

"Oh my God, what am I to do?"

"Sit down, my child, and listen. Your comfort gone, you will listen now to mine. You have hit the bottom of the rock, you hurt, and you are in despair. But this rock is the substance of the earth, it is her life beneath your feet, her love that is sustaining and supporting you.

"Dressed in the rags of your health and your wealth and your status in society gone with the wind, you sit before me and finally you listen. Broken is the bulwark of your defenses against me and all I have created for you. At last will you allow me to reach your heart?

"You cannot come to me but empty handed. Stretch out your hands and I will fill them with a wealth, as you have never known.

"Open wide your eyes that have been closed so long and I will show you what you have never seen: a world your friend, humanity your family, and the Identity I gave you in exchange for the one you made.

"Through the thin layers of your rags, you will feel my warm embrace.

"You will receive your food from the hands of those around you; know it is my gift.

"Allow other hands to care for you and know that they are mine.

"You need do nothing but receive. And as in gratitude you learn that you are love, you will know yourself and me.

"I Am that I Am,
I am all I created; I am the other; I am you.
Be still and know that I am God—and so are you.

I Am that I Am,
I am all I created; I am the other, and I am you.
Be still and know that I am God—in you, my home."

The more we find our divine Identity, the more we can assist others to discover theirs, and increase the harmony in which we all can grow.

God, expressing himself as our life and love, touches and heals all. And there is a powerful way to bring forth and share God's power in us that is knocking to be let out, every moment in our life.

Let us close our eyes and imagine the planet with all that lives on it to exist within us. Six billion people, the whole of humanity, with the full range of their happiness and suffering, live in our mind. And all we need to do is, in prayer, cover all living creatures, all places, as well as past and future with the blanket of our love.

We have God's promise that, in time, wholeness will prevail over suffering and evil, because the love that is inspiring us to do this, is the everlasting reality of God.

We are always on our way to that happiness, and the art of living is to be content with what it takes to get us there.

There is a divine moment for being content. It contains all of the future and the healing of the past. This divine moment is now. There is a holy place too. It is here!

The past is gone; the future is not here. There is nowhere to go and nowhere to be but now and here. This makes every place and every moment sacred. Not only the past was holy when Jesus, Buddha, Ramah, Mohammed, or Guru Nanak were on earth, nor the future when we die and go to heaven or when Christ will fully have returned on earth in human hearts. The sacred time is now and the sacred place is here, with you and me walking the earth and living our life in the full range of its experiences.

Every moment is holy. We learn about ourselves when we are low, and our longing to be high again creates the momentum to rise. We are unhappy when we are not in harmony with planetary, social, or moral order and we feel we are not at the right time in the right place. These moments reflect back to us who we are and what we truly want, and reveal our inner creative resources with which to rectify the situation.

Every situation is holy. Each problem is a challenge to our creativity. All resistance is the opportunity to bring forth the highest in us.

In our life-long experiment with opposites, we learn from their effects and gather wisdom. How would we know harmony if that were all there is? How could we love it, yearn for it, and do everything we can to find it when we have lost it? In disharmony we learn of our desire for harmony, and we get to know the power of our creativity when we desperately work our way back into that blessed state. In the process, we realize our strength to overcome hurdles on our path and to conquer the world—with love.

At peace with ourselves, we recreate peace on earth even when we vacuum the house, browse the shelves of the supermarket or repair the car. And when we are not at peace, we are in the sacred process of recreating it.

To be unhappy and out of harmony, to feel wronged, angered, or victimized, is sacred as well as being happy, fulfilled, and creative. Our saga is about working our way from babyhood to mature old age and death, from feeling unhappy to being contented, from bringing disharmony to harmony and back. This creates our history, and makes us ask each other,

"How are you? What has happened? Tell me the story!"

We travel from dark to light, from density to clarity, and when all possibilities are exhausted within the context of our lives, we go home with our stories. And maybe, just maybe, we may like to come back to earth one day, to create a new saga and manifest our source in a new painting of life.

> I bless you Lord from the depth
> Of my light and my darkness,
> My littleness and my grandeur,
> My perfection and my imperfection,
> My love and my lack of love.
> I bless you from the abyss of my loneliness,
> And on the mountaintops of the glory
> Of being one with you.

A few blessed religions celebrate God's importance as a child, in remembrance of our toddler state of innocence, joy, and unlimited possibilities.

In India, Hindu devotees still tell each other the delightful pranks and miracles of little Lord Krishna, the pure God Consciousness in form, who lived on earth over five thousand years ago. In the temple corner in Indian homes, there is always a picture of the adorable toddler with the bluish complexion—his skin was so white that it seemed to be blue. His pitch-black hair is tied in a knot on top of his sweet head; his neck is decorated with a garland of orange flowers and he lifts a chubby hand in blessing. The devotees lovingly hang a garland with sweet smelling flowers on the picture and, during prayers, they burn incense to make the air itself around him holy. Adoration of toddler Lord Krishna reflects back on the Indian children even today.

To Christians through the ages, the infant Jesus has been the object of their most tender devotion. Each year in December, millions of people, regardless of whether they are Christians or not, celebrate the birth of baby Jesus two thousand years ago. To whatever extent—it may be nothing more than the child-like joy of receiving a present—all respond to the appeal of his authority of God, living in an innocent baby that has the world at his delicate fingertips.

Unfortunately, no endearing portrait of him in stories has been left to us. What a wisdom-filled, glorious bubble of joy he must have been!

One of the stories might have been like this:

Costyn was ten years old at the time. Kenya—known as a wildlife paradise—had attracted a rich businessman from the United Sates. Mr. Jones had bought a ranch with thousands of acres of semi-arid land, teeming with wildlife, and its luxurious mansion that had been built by some rich Arab sheik.

In the hot climate, he and his overseas guests would need to refresh themselves in a swimming pool, so he needed a lot of extra water, and Pieter was asked to do the survey. Luckily, there appeared to be enough groundwater available to supply the necessary quantity. In due time a borehole was made and a pump got installed. The experts explained Mr. Jones' staff how everything worked

Then the problems began. The manager of the ranch kept calling Pieter to complain that too little water was forthcoming, that the water was brackish, or that there was no water at all. Several times more, he or his colleagues went back there—five hours drive over the most appalling roads—only to find that the staff still did not work the machinery properly and had to be shown the procedure again.

When it all appeared to have been sorted out, one day Mr. Big Shot called. He was in a rage. The water for the swimming pool was dirty; he did not have water even in the house, and there he was expecting his important friends from the States in a few days time.

He had taken his inner war with the world to the peace of his African property and the people who took care of it, and he shouted, "I'll sue you for a million shillings!"

Pieter's company was beginning to take off, but this was a considerable amount of money at the time, and it would mean the end of it all. Knowing that the water was available, he put the phone down, grinned, and said,

"Oh well, then we'll be bankrupt, so let's have a beer!"

Of course, he sent his best expert there straightaway, and all he found was that the staff still did not understand how to work the pump.

A few days later, we were talking about this at the breakfast table. Costyn had finished eating and got up to get ready to go to school. While he walked out of the room, Pieter, still annoyed at all the time consuming, unnecessary work the man was creating, concluded the morning's discussion,

"Mr. Jones does not deserve water!"

The child heard this. He stopped in his tracks. He turned around and, the wrath of God's justice shining in his eyes, he declared, "Of course Mr. Jones deserves water! He is a child of God, too!"

On that, he stalked off. Over the toast and marmalade, we looked at each other, speechless and ashamed.

"Ouch!" we finally brought out.

What else was left to say?

If only we could become like a child again and once more believe that life is magic; approach it with the innocence of a toddler, with every moment new and exciting, created from the Now!

It is hard. At times, life is so burdened that it seems too heavy to bear. We have been hurt too often and we expect the future to be no different from the past. We have closed our heart long ago and we have lost the key. Can we ever open it again?

Deep within, we long to be that trusting joy, this adorable defenselessness again, to be friend to others and to God and to love ourselves.

It is within our power to change the way our heart feels, for a change of heart is nothing but a change of mind. We can even make a beginning with it today, if we want.

We can decide to let down our defenses and, out of the blue, unconditionally, and without any reason—especially without reason—smile at someone whose eyes we happen to meet; to do this again tomorrow and the day after. Then we get bold and, for an entire day, smile at everyone we meet, whether we feel like it or not. A smile, which holds no judgment and that says, "I accept you as you are, and you are lovable."

We will see a shine appear on the face of the other that warms our heart, and these moments of defenselessness bring back the shine on our own as we begin to feel how dearly we, too, are loved. It seems so small, but it is not. We change the other, the world, and ourselves. That shine is God.

Jesus says,

"Where two or more are gathered in my name, I am in their midst.

"I, the infinite divine Consciousness, am telling you: my name is love. Where love is, I am. I AM is love."

Our heart knows the mind of God. Our mind knows our heart, if we allow it. We do, when we are a child—if we are allowed.

One day I was in bed with a sinus infection. I had a temperature and my head was hurting badly. Our little one, three years old, entered the room and when he saw me miserable and in pain, he knelt down on the floor next to my head. He put his chubby hand, still dirty from playing in the garden with water and sand, on my forehead and looked at me with those eyes in which the whole of the cosmos was still visible. He said,

"Through my little hand, Jesus puts his hand on your forehead now."

Immediately the pain left as if someone was pulling it out on a string, and it never returned. The meek hold heaven and earth in the hollow of their hand. Sweet child, you are a smile of God!

All children of creation are in the hollow of the Father's hand. As we keep them safe in our love, let them be our teachers and show us the strength of innocence, vulnerability, and trust. Let them gently guide us back to remembering that love holds us safe and protected too. And when we nurture trust as it returns in us through them, it will flower to its full potential.

We are so loved. We are so holy. Let us honor ourselves for who we are: Christ-Son-Daughter of Father-Mother God.

We are the toddlers of the universe; our essence is innocence, spontaneity, and creativity. We are love clothed in matter.

We carry the heart of God within our own, and thus our heart is the ruler of the universe. It sings,

"We are big
And God is small,
I love you all!"

Royal Rooster!

He was truly magnificent!

Two feet tall he stood, from comb to heel.

Shall I describe him from top to bottom, or the other way round?

He had strong feet with long nails and stood high on powerful legs, armed with vicious spurs. His body was shiny coal-black with long feathers cascading down his sides. At the rear end, a magnificent tail expressed royalty. It fanned out in metallic blue and green, in brown and white. The comb was yellowish orange, the eyes a fierce yellow, and the big beak light brown.

He was the king of the compound and proud master of ten wives.

Let me tell you first why I had this sweet lot as part of my extended farm-family.

On a pleasant afternoon, a bit cloudy and not too hot, we had tea with friends who had a farm in the Athi Plains, outside Nairobi. It was a large ranch of semi-arid land that was still full of wildlife, and the veranda where we sat had a magnificent wide view over the plains where gazelles darted around and zebras grazed contentedly.

In the distance, four or five giraffes had a meal off the top of an acacia tree. In all my years in Africa, these animals have never ceased to amaze me. They are like appearances from prehistoric times. When you drive through a game park or through scarcely populated savannah land, you may be surprised by a giraffe peeking through the trees at the side of the road. You stop. You look. You look up; and up, and even higher. Finally, halfway to the sky, you see a rather small head with lovely pointed ears, crowned by knobby horns that always seem about to be growing into real ones, and you look into the meekest, softest brown eyes. They stare at you as if they are seeing the oddest animal ever, and while you wonder who has come to see whom, you feel like offering them your camera.

To watch them gallop away takes you out of this world. In utter slow motion, they thrust their long neck forward and effortlessly throw themselves fully up in the air. They stay suspended for a while, and then come down to lightly touch the ground and repeat the movement. Their mighty bodies seem to be flying without wings.

Our friends on the ranch did not experience them quite that way. The heads of the giraffes are so elevated that they don't see the telephone wires when they gallop. They were forever breaking them, and getting a telephone repaired in Kenya is a saga in itself.

We were given the tour of the farm. It was very interesting to see how a farm functions in a semi-arid area, but when we came to the chicken houses, my happy mood collapsed. Thousands of poultry were being kept in endless rows of cages, which each held two chickens in a space for one. The bottoms were wired so that the droppings could fall through, and this meant that the chickens had to spend the whole of their short, miserable existence, day and night holding on to steel wires. Their only excuse for life was the eggs they dropped into a kind of gutter on the outside along the cages, but once they lost their productivity they were slaughtered. It made me so sick at heart that I decided there and then that I would never have an egg from a store again, and I started my own chicken family.

In our quest for the living God, we become aware of many things. I realized that, if I ate fertilized eggs, I was killing potential life. The easy way out of that one was not to have a rooster. Or so I thought, but the Universe did not agree.

When they want to honor someone, Africans like to present a rooster. This means sharing food, which is a precious commodity for many, and it is out of the question to refuse. Whenever we received one, I could not kill or eat it, of course, and so my hens always had a Man in their lives! According to the wishes of the Universe there was a full life for everyone—except for the embryos, of course.

We had made the chicken pen in the shade of a jacaranda tree. Three sides were chicken wire, the fourth a tall impenetrable kei-apple hedge under which they could hide from humans who wanted to take the eggs they were planning to hatch, or from the birds of prey.

A noisy panic broke out in the chicken pen, once in a while, when black kites, or even hawks and eagles circled the sky above, preying upon the chicks or a young hen for breakfast.

One morning, a tremendous uproar among the fowl was joined by the voices of the gardeners. One of the biggest birds of prey, an Augur Buzzard, had dived inside the pen. The hen he had tried to catch had made for the hedge and he had missed her, but in the process he had come down too low to have enough space to take off again. In desperate panic he was clinging at the mesh. When I arrived at the scene, Jacob, one of the gardeners, had just managed to grab him and he was prying loose the claws. As he proudly held the bird up in a position that it could neither bite him nor fly away, I asked if he was going to release it somewhere down the slope. Bewildered, he answered:

"Release it? I'll kill it, of course."

"What! Kill this magnificent bird?"

"It is eating our chickens."

"Let it go!"

"No! It will come back again. I'm going to kill it!"

Feelings started running high.

"Take it down the slope immediately and set it free!"

I was the boss, so my will had to be done and reluctantly he went, with a pitiful look at me, 'The woman has gone out of her mind!'

Well, he was right. She had gone out of her mind, into her heart.

The higher part of the garden was sloping gently down into the valley. It consisted of an acre of grass, with here and there a tree and a flowerbed. It was separated by a hedge from the lower part, which was another acre of jungle leading down to the river.

We were all occupied with our peaceful afternoon business, one day, including King Rooster and his harem. Under his watchful eye, the hens had wandered off down the slope, scratching and pecking the soil.

Suddenly the afternoon quiet was torn apart by the rooster screeching at the top of his voice. We all stopped dead in our tracks and listened. As I rushed out of the house, followed by my two ladies, the gardeners were storming down the hill. Even the mechanics had dropped their tools and came running.

We did not see the chickens anywhere but, in a fury larger than life, the rooster was running up and down along the hedge. He had chased his hens underneath for cover, and flapping his mighty wings and yelling at the top of his voice, he was holding off two huge birds of prey circling over his head! The gardeners came to his rescue and, with shouts and stones, they chased away the birds, which flew off under loud protest.

We were all speechless with admiration. This animal had taken on two enemies, each one much bigger than he, himself. They could easily have torn him to pieces with their terrible beaks and claws, but, in order to protect his wives, he had overcome his instinct of self-preservation. Armed with nothing but his willpower and his courage, he had held the two enemies high in the sky.

Finally, gardener Jonathan proudly said, "A real African man!"

We women giggled.

The garden was a true delicatessen for the chickens. Tidbits of worm, ant, and insect were just a scratch deep away. The rooster, usually followed by one or two of his favorite ladies, did his own survey. Every now and then he clucked a special sound in the back of his throat, which made the hens come running from far and near. This was the signal that he had found something very tasty.

And while they pecked excitedly at whatever it was, the patriarch stood aside and kept watch without making any effort to get his share. He had provided and he was content.

If there was anything left after they finished, he ate it. If not, he calmly walked on in search of the next opportunity to sound his chuckle, make them eat, and have something himself, or not.

A few days later, my friend Janet came to visit me. She has a highly developed gift of seeing, hearing, and understanding in finer realms of consciousness to which the day-to-day senses do not have access. Thanks to her extra- sensorial perception, we were often blessed with deeper spiritual insights into what was happening in our lives.

I told her how this animal's soul was as splendid as his appearance.

"The greater part of humanity could learn from him!" I concluded my story passionately.

At that moment, she saw—and I sensed—our beloved Indian spiritual guide Sathya Sai Baba appear.

"Because you have understood this, the rooster can now move into a higher state of consciousness," he said.

We looked at each other, perplexed,

"Did we hear this right?"

"You did!"

Slowly we tried to figure out the meaning of this amazing statement. I said to Janet:

"Humans are in an upward movement toward a higher state of consciousness. It must be the same for other life forms. What do you think?"

"Ideally human consciousness is the highest expression of divine Mind on the planet," Janet mused. "And ultimately all individual life is linked together in the All-Consciousness, in God."

We looked at the animals around us. The dogs were lying at our feet; here and there in the garden a cat was curled up in the cool sand under the plants, and the parrot was having his siesta. They all depended on us and they all loved us. Their minds and their feelings connected them with ours, with our consciousness.

"So where we grow, all grow," I concluded.

Tufe got up, our Japanese Spitz, a white, longhaired dog with slightly slanted eyes. He was so elegant on his slender legs that a friend who saw him for the first time, burst out laughing and said, "That's not a dog, that is a cross between a ballet dancer and a cat!"

He smelled something in the air. He walked to the fishpond and, turned toward the backyard and the neighbors, stood very still. For a long while, only his nose was moving as he sniffed in all directions.

"Look Janet!" I said. "He is reading the Neighborhood Daily. All the news comes in through his nose."

This suddenly made her see the essence of what we were trying to understand.

"Now that your and my consciousness know and verbally express how he gathers his information, dog-consciousness is expressed in the human one. I think this is the way in which we are a window to higher consciousness for other life-forms."

"I can see how a dog, trained to be a guide dog, in close companionship with a human being expands his awareness of the world," I agreed. "An animal, which has learned enough to be able to take responsibility for the life of a blind person, is a very different creature from the one who has it easy and does not grow beyond his instincts of eating, walking and sleeping—maybe guarding—and a natural affection. A street dog's existence is restricted to surviving and mating, and he will not be challenged to go beyond his most direct instincts. A lone survivor without anyone to share love and affection with, he cannot develop a more independent intelligence, nor grow in selfless love."

"Our respectful, loving relationship with them allows other life forms to grow in life-intelligence," Janet concluded.

This rooster had left behind all selfishness. There was no greed in him and he seemed to have risen above his instincts. He gave before he took, and his instinct of self-preservation had been transformed into sheer courage, as we all had witnessed when he demonstrated that he did not hesitate to risk his life to protect the weaker ones.

He had learned all there is to learn on earth within the fowl consciousness. His life-intelligence had developed to a degree that there was no more room for further growth and since life is expansion, this particular one had to come to an end. The intelligence, which was this rooster, could only evolve further if it moved into a higher life form with new possibilities of expression.

My human consciousness had recognized and expressed the rooster's state of being and, as a blind person is a gateway to a higher life-intelligence for a guide dog, I had become one for this animal.

"Baba, what is going to be his next form?"

"What would you like?"

"Let me see... he has to be close to humans again. Let him come back as a dog," I said.

"Ah, no!" I corrected myself. "As a cat, of course! For cats, even closed doors are no obstacles to be with humans day and night; if they want to sleep on our bed, they can jump in through the bedroom window."

Baba smiled and left, and we delighted in some more speculations on how and where and when this might happen.

The rooster got a swelling on his leg. We put extra vitamin powder in his food to enhance his resistance, but he became ill and listless.

I put him in a box and took him to the vet.

The vet shook her sweet head and gave him an injection.

No sign of improvement.

I took him back and he got another injection. He did not get any better.

Then Sai Baba gave me the opportunity to talk with him again.

"Baba, what is going on, what else can I do for him?"

"His earth-cycle in the present consciousness is finished. You can carry on like this if you want, but you only prolong his suffering."

This message was clear, but it was as hard to see him suffering as it was to take the decision to let him die.

After a few days, the poor animal became so miserable that I could not stand it any longer. I put him in the box again, took him to the vet and explained her everything.

"Let us put him to sleep; let him come back in a beautiful new body," I asked her.

She was a Hindu lady, deeply devoted to God, and life ending and coming back into a new form was a familiar concept to her. Nevertheless, torn between her heart that told her that she should keep trying, and her reason, which knew that there was nothing more she could do, she always found it an extremely difficult task to finish a life. However, we both had tried everything we could, and together we decided to end his suffering.

She cried.

I cried.

The rooster was gone.

The Universe brought me comfort, this time in the shape of a baby parrot. The poor thing was so young when I got it, that it could not even crack the sunflower seeds. We had to peel them, crush them up, chew them a bit, and put them in its beak.

Janet came to see the new treasure. She loved it. She bent over it, crooning, calling it sweet names and making little whistling noises for it to imitate—which, of course, it could not do yet. I had put the bird close to us in a portable cage, and we kept looking at it while we talked. All of a sudden, it began to shiver. I put a cloth over the side of the cage where the wind came from, and while we watched it anxiously, its feathers began to droop under our very eyes. Soon, the poor little thing could hardly keep its head up. I took it out of the cage and gave it to Janet. It felt hot.

She held it against her heart; she stroked it and softly talked to it. I joined in with my own love for the little creature, and God's love in all its beauty was flowing around us, in us, and through us to the little bird.

Janet became aware of the presence of Master Luke, he who wrote the Bible Gospel of Luke and is considered to have been a physician. He told us that the animal was born with a hole in its windpipe and could not live.

After Janet had left, I took the bird inside the house. A few hours later, it lay dead at the bottom of the cage.

Brutally taken from its nest for financial gain when it was too young even to eat on its own, it had soon ended a life that could not have lasted anyway. However, in accordance with the cosmic law of love attracting love, it had found its mysterious way to us, and in the loving hands of two women, this traumatized wild animal being had been lifted up into the human divine love-consciousness. What more was there to it that we will never know?

A few months later, friends came over for dinner. They handed me a box. I opened it, and to my surprise there were two tiny mouse-gray kittens inside. They were not more than four weeks old, too young to leave their mother, really.

"For you!" the friends radiated.

We already had five cats. Cats are lonely hunters, each with their own domain in which they do not tolerate any intrusion, and whenever I brought a new cat into to the house, even if it was a kitten, the others usually became nasty and cruel. And these two were far too small to defend themselves.

The farmhouse had about forty doors and windows for the big cats to sneak in, so it would involve the constant effort of everybody in the household to keep the kittens locked in and protected until they were big enough to fight back and conquer their own terrain. As if life was not complicated enough already!

I held them both in one hand, the ones to be called Shiva and Shakti.

"I hate you!" I told the friends, everything in me shining with delight.

Some time later, we sat on Janet's veranda. She had thrown a handful of seeds for the birds and we watched them, fascinated by the quick, light movements of the excited crowd of little seedeaters, her pets. I told her about the arrival of the kittens.

Sai Baba came.

"You know them," he said, with a smile expressing, 'I have a nice surprise for you!'

"Oh! Which ones may have come back to me in a new life?" I wondered happily, and I went through all the cats I remembered from early childhood onward. All of a sudden, I clapped my hands and exclaimed, "I know, I know!"

"What, what is it?"

"I know, I know!" Too excited to explain, I finally managed to bring out,

"One of them has to be King Rooster!"

We laughed with delight and we puzzled, "Now, which one would he be, the male or the female kitten?"

My heart whispered, "The other one is the little parrot," and from there it was easy.

"Shakti should be the parrot then!" The memory of the problem, which had cost the little parrot its life, had cast a harmless shadow over the present one. "This little girl-kitten cannot purr properly," I told her.

"So Shiva is the rooster," Janet said. "How amazing!"

"Imagine," I added, "he could have been born anywhere in the world; I never expected him to come back here, with us."

Where to draw the fine line between delighted fantasy and creative inspiration? Does it matter? It is the joy that counts.

Shakti lived her first cat incarnation sure in her instincts and pure in her heart. Sweet and innocent she was. It was fascinating to see how she took care of her kittens when she got her first litter. We take instinct for granted, but as this was her first experience of cat-motherhood after having been a bird, I was filled with wonder and profound respect. How did she know it all?

All cats have something that makes them different from any other cat. One talks to you all the time; another expresses his annoyance by turning his back to you after you have been away, and a third one walks over the piano when she is hungry.

For many years I had a tomcat that punished me relentlessly whenever he was seriously annoyed with me—usually when I brought home another cat. He used to pee where it hurt most: in the socket with the telephone connection, causing a short circuit that made normal conversation impossible; against the walls of my prayer room, where he had to jump uncomfortably high to get in; in my paint box with all the tubes; against an oil painting that was still wet; over the crystals, and in the packed suitcase ready to be taken to the airport. If I dared scold him, his inscrutable eyes looked at me in cold innocence, conveying the message that I was the one who had Crossed the Line.

Shiva did not live very long. In our ignorance, we had had him neutered and he disappeared after not even two years. Desperately, we searched the neighborhood far and wide for days, but in my heart I understood what had happened. Just like the chickens, he had needed a full life and he would return in circumstances in which he could experience one.

His cat-personality really had been new. It had been blank. He had been a cat as cats are, sweet, independent, and self-willed and that was it. He had no tricks to show of understanding the exquisite game of manipulating humans!

He had been beautiful, though, with his sleek, shining gray fur. He had had a small triangular face with alert and watchful eyes, yellow-green and perfectly round, as if he was living in a constant state of surprise. And he may well have been. With his tail high up in the air, he had proudly walked the compound, tall on his long legs.

Shiva—A tomcat truly magnificent!

Mwangi, Little Mwangi

Viju looked absolutely regal in her flaming red sari, its borders embroidered with gold. Her transparent gold-flecked green eyes were most striking in her fine Indian face, set off against the heavy mass of her black hair, which she wore gathered in a knot at the nape of her neck. Golden earrings and golden bangles on her arms completed this beautiful picture.

I was wearing a Punjabi suit—this traditional Indian costume that consists of a dress, flaring out over wide baggy trousers that are gathered at the ankles. It was white, printed with bronze colored plant motifs, and made of fine handspun linen, the way Gandhi taught the people in his time of revolt against British industrial imperialism.

We would go to the temple at eleven o'clock. It was the special day of the Mother Goddess Durga, who is also known as Parvati, the consort of Lord Shiva, the destroyer of our obstacles to God. With their two sons Ganesha and Kartikeya, they manifest the ideal of family unity and love.

Her priests were going to perform a fire ceremony in the open hall in the front part of the temple. In a specially constructed concrete pit, they would place a fire pot and feed the flames with sandalwood and incense, all the while chanting mantras to bless the devotees with their prayers

Viju was staying with us for a few weeks. The family was leaving the country for good and her husband had already gone back to India, but she wanted some time for herself. Over the many years they had lived in Kenya, she had been deeply involved in welfare work. She had 'adopted' a complete starving village in the dry, eastern province of Kenya, and organized food, medical aid, and education for the villagers, all by her sweet self. The people had honored her by adopting her in return. They had given her her own hut and compound. From their meager possessions, they had donated goats and chickens, so that she had livestock as it should be, and they always took care that she had her vegetarian food in maize, beans, and millet. It was difficult to say farewell for all involved, and a constant stream of people kept coming to our house to see her one last time.

This morning was no different. We were ready, and so was Gideon, the driver who was going to take us to the temple, but visitor after visitor delayed us. Much later than we had planned, we finally managed to get the last one out by offering him a lift to town, and we left.

We drove along the dirt road between the trees and descended the steep slope of our hill over badly broken tarmac. The main road at the bottom folded itself left and right around the valley and, like most roads of Nairobi, was in a deplorable state, too. The tarmac was broken at the sides. There were huge potholes. In one place, the Nairobi city council water was flowing freely from a broken pipe, and this leak caused a crater lake in the middle of the road, which took two years before it got repaired!

Either turn, right or left, would take us to town, but as the right side was virtually impassable, we always turned left.

Gideon began his usual left turn, but in a sudden impulse I said: "No, go right, please!"

Surprised, he turned the wheel, and on we went, swerving around the potholes. On our left side was the deep valley; on our right the slope went steeply uphill. About five hundred meters farther down there was a path, cut by erosion, going up between the eucalyptus trees. This was a shortcut to school for the children who came from Mwimuto, a village two kilometers farther along the road. Around seven in the morning, they could be seen climbing up, and at four in the afternoon, tired and hungry, they came down again to walk all the way back home.

When we came to this spot, I saw three boys coming down, in gray sweaters and blue shorts, the school uniform. Two seemed to support the smaller one in the middle who clearly could not walk. He was holding his left foot up in the air and the others were half carrying him.

Our minds were on our destination, so it took a moment before I realized that this was altogether the wrong time for them to be there and that they still had desperately far to go with that little boy hopping on one foot.

"Gideon, please stop! Something is wrong there; let's find out."

Gideon reversed, put the car on the side of the road and got out. I followed him.

The boy was about ten years old, the other two a bit older. He looked ill. He said that he had hurt his toe in the morning, but clearly there was more wrong with him. The older boys told us that he had a dreadful headache and since he could not walk properly, the headmaster had told them to take the little one home. Ill, walking, hopping for two kilometers... A poor solution from a poor school.

It was clear to all of us that we had to do something and we decided to take the child to Mwimuto where he lived. We asked the extra passenger to kindly get out of the car and take the matatu—a minibus—to town. One boy went back to school and the other one came with us, along with the patient. Gideon turned the car around in the opposite direction from the temple and the fire ceremony and we were on our way to the dispensary in his village to see what needed to be done.

In villages all over Africa, there are small health centers with a medical officer or a nurse and a small pharmacy, where many of the common health problems can be taken care of locally. Doctors are rare and hospitals expensive and often far away, so on the whole this solution works quite well.

After ten minutes of slalom driving around even deeper potholes, while at the same time trying not to be hit by the oncoming reckless matatus that were doing the same thing at high speed, we reached the village. The dispensary was close to the road, but to reach it we had to perform a deep dive off the broken edge of the tarmac, careful not to rip open the bottom of the car.

Fortunately the nurse was in. She put the child on a bed to examine him, and the other boy was asked to go and fetch its mother.

"He doesn't have a mother, she has left," the boy told us. "His father has gone off to work, but I can ask the neighbor to come."

"You just do that; we need an adult here who knows him and can take responsibility," we urged him on.

The nurse took little Mwangi's temperature. It was extremely high. The headache made Viju and me worry that he had meningitis, but according to her, the symptoms were different. She thought it was cerebral malaria. In any case, it was clear that he urgently needed to be taken to a hospital. As his father would not come home before evening, this would mean a dangerous delay of at least seven hours. Even then, he would have to take the child to the hospital in a matatu, ill as he was.

Viju and I looked at each other. No words were needed; of course we would not leave him there to die.

The other boy returned with a young woman, Mwangi's neighbor. We explained the situation and asked her if she could come with us to Kikuyu Hospital, some twenty kilometers farther inland. She agreed, bless her, and went home to put her own small child in the care of a friend.

Mwangi was only half-conscious by then, and Gideon had to carry him back into the car. Viju and the neighbor sat in the back and held Mwangi between them, with the child half-sitting, half-lying over their laps. His breathing was difficult and irregular and he felt so hot!

In Gideon, God had provided us with an extra guardian Angel. He was gentle and always friendly, and God was as familiar to him as breathing in and out. He knew the way to the hospital and he calmly drove us to our destination.

In the back of the car, Viju was praying over the child and I did the same in my front seat. I talked to God, "Lord, this is your child. You love him as your own; he is yours and he has never been anything else. Let nothing happen that is not your will."

Now and then I looked back. Mwangi's breathing was getting shallow and jerky.

My prayer became more intense, "Dear God, Ground of our being, we bring you your child. Hold him in your light and love. Let nothing but your will be done!"

All of a sudden a great peace folded itself around me. It seemed to come out of the blue sky in front of us and I knew then that all was well. He would either live and get better, or die and go Home.

We reached the country hospital, a simple wooden structure. It was run by American and English missionary doctors, and it had an excellent reputation.

Gideon carried Mwangi to Emergency and laid him on a bed. After some anxious talking back and forth in Kikuyu language, one of the nurses went out to call a doctor.

We looked around. The room was dark and shabby and it had been a long time since it had seen any paint. It was so small that there was hardly space for all of us, but Viju and I were given a creaking wooden chair and we sat down close to the bed.

It was an amazing scene of contrasts. Viju looked like a queen in her flamboyant red and golden sari, and I, a white person— a Mzungu—was wearing a white Indian dress. There also was the neighbor lady, and a very round nurse, both Africans—all of us gathered around a dying Kikuyu child on a bed in an upcountry emergency room.

His fever was so high that he seemed to radiate heat, and he was hardly breathing. We waited for the doctor and continued to pray.

A Kikuyu doctor came rushing in. He looked at the boy, he listened to his chest, and then, to our amazement, he began to talk to him. He did not order the nurses into high activity, nor did he give the child anti-malarial and antibiotic injections, which is always the first thing they do.

He asked us, "What is his name?"

"Mwangi, doctor."

Bent over the child, he talked Kikuyu in a very intense way. I don't know the language, so I could not understand anything, except for the English word 'cemetery', which came upover and over again. I thought, 'What, for heaven's sake, is this man doing, talking about the cemetery to a dying child?'

He kept calling his name, "Mwangi! Mwangi!" and never ceased talking until, finally, the boy began to moan. At that moment the doctor turned around and declared,

"He will be all right now!"

Only then he gave his instructions to the nurse and he handed us a prescription for medication that we could buy from the hospital pharmacy.

"I'll be back in a little while," he promised and left.

I went in search of the pharmacy. It was around midday and there was a long line waiting. With my white skin and my Indian finery, I felt like an exotic bird among the Kikuyu, but they were very friendly and interested, and the half hour I had to wait for my turn passed quickly. Gideon, who had not come inside with us, saw me. I told him how close the child had been to dying, what the doctor had done, and how Mwangi had responded. He, in turn, told me how moved everyone was that we two ladies, Indian and European, had found this poor, sick African child on the road and taken care of him.

I felt happy and honored. God had used us to demonstrate that his love works in everyone who is willing to listen, regardless of color, race, creed, or status in life.

When I finally returned to the ward, I heard with regret that I had missed the doctor. He had come, sat for a while, and explained how he had performed an ancient ritual.

"This is the way we do it traditionally," he had said, "I called on Mwangi's forefathers of the same name."

In the Bantu-African belief system, we form one uninterrupted line of life with our ancestors and even with the ones to be born. The Kikuyu always name their first son after the father of the man so that the grandfather will live on in the child. As long as a person is present in the consciousness of someone on earth, he is one with the living one of the same name. He does not cease to exist and can continue to perform his task of being a spiritual guide and guardian of his lineage.

The doctor had called on the collective ancestral Mwangi and demanded,

"Mwangi! I claim your help. I claim this life. You have to give back to us this dying child!" And the ancient tribal Kikuyu soul of little Mwangi had responded where any other medical activity would have failed.

We could take Mwangi home. Weak and dazed, but with less pain and fever, he walked out of the hospital on his own two feet, supported by Gideon. We took him back to his house where the neighbor promised to take care of him until his father would come home.

The next day we told our story to Janet. She was deeply moved, and became aware of Sai Baba. Viju and I could not 'see' him the way she did but we could sense the power and the love of his Presence.

"I was that doctor!" he declared. "The child was dying and the only way to save his life was to claim him back from his ancestors in the ancient way."

We were stunned. We knew that he manifests himself in whatever form is needed to come to the rescue of those who love him, but it was so hard to believe that this was happening to us. How low was our self-esteem that we could not accept that God loves us enough to want to be with us and assist us in whatever we try to do out of our love for him?

"The boy was already ill in the morning," Baba continued, "but in his heart I ordered him to go to school, otherwise he would have died alone in the house."

"The father will take better care of his children from now on," was his final statement. And that was good to hear. From this auspicious day of the Mother Goddess onward, the family bond would be tightened and the children would know themselves more protected.

Some days later, a friend came by, a European medical specialist who had worked in hospitals in Nairobi for many years. He knew Sai Baba too; he was reading his books and, like us, he was trying to follow the path to inner peace that Baba indicates.

I told him the story. His eyes became very big, and with great intensity he said, "It has to be him! No African doctor, trained in western medicine, would resort to the old traditional practices in this way—ever!"

This was another confirmation that Baba had meant that he had saved the child. The Kikuyu doctor by himself, or the highly trained Western doctors would have been powerless to hold back this child who had been slipping away fast. Only a miracle could have held him here and love had provided it!

I have often wondered about little Mwangi. I never felt the urge to follow it up and I never saw him again. Gideon passed him by once, in the same place where we had found him.

"He looked very well," he beamed.

What memory lingers in the child's mind? In his high fever he must have seen two apparitions, one in red and one in white.

Did he see Angels while he was dying? Is he wondering if he dreamt it all? Does he know?

I still thank God for the split second, in which I gave in to the irrational urge to turn right instead of left. I might never have heard of a child who died on the Mwimuto road, but the experience had evolved into a cosmic event that had enriched the souls of all involved. His deep pain of rejection had been healed when, in the time-honored tradition of his people, he had been reminded of his belonging to the community of ancestors and their living lineage on earth and he had chosen life over death.

We are bound in love forever. When love of the heart answers a call from the soul, they meet in paradise.

Viju and I had celebrated our own fire ceremony in the burning fever, which had been consuming the child. Under the auspices of Durga, the Mother Goddess, the female aspect of God, we had been mother to little Mwangi, who did not have one. We, both of us a mother, had been instrumental in reclaiming the life that she had once given and thrown away.

We ourselves had been the priestesses.

And we had dressed for God.

Oh yes, we had!

Love on Prescription

"How are you doing?" Max inquired. "These roads are no joke even for a healthy back! Mine sure feels stiff!"

For the past four years I had been suffering with a serious back problem, but that could not keep me home when there was a fantastic safari with good friends on the program. We were on our way to Turkana, in northern Kenya. The best roads were full of potholes, the worst virtually nonexistent, and for the past three hours we had been traveling on the latter. On the worst stretch, Pieter had stacked a couple of mattresses on the bed in the camper, and I had traveled laying down, level with the window, and enjoyed the scenery and the wild animals without any pressure on my spine.

We had arrived at Lake Bogoria, a shallow Rift Valley soda lake, one of nature's great marvels at the foot of the Laikipia escarpment. As always, our hearts had skipped a beat the moment we reached the top of the escarpment, where the view opened on a volcanically active lake with water in a delicate hue of green-blue. About a million flamingo color long stretches of the shores pink and white, and steam jets and geysers, which spout in the thermal areas, enliven the Western end.

The lake has no outlet, and the evaporation that is caused by the equatorial heat has led to high levels of salt and minerals, in which green algae, spirulina, grow in abundance. These are the ideal nourishment for the deep pink Lesser Flamingo and the nearly white Greater Flamingo. At a few spots along the shores, fresh water flows into the lake and provides drinking water for the birds and other wildlife.

Dominated by the bluish hills of the towering Laikipia escarpment and with a blessed absence of tourist accommodation, the lake is of a dramatic and primeval beauty. Untouched and unchanged since the time of its creation, its silence conveys eternity.

We had made our camp at the southern end of the lake, at Fig Tree Camp, an exquisite spot where a mass of giant figs create an oasis of coolness and green in the landscape of mainly dry bush, grass, and rocks. A small stream, flowing down from its source higher up the hillside, provided drinking water and, further downstream, a natural pool for the children to play.

Max was a medical specialist, a dedicated idealist who worked among the poorest of the poor in a small hospital somewhere deep inland.

"Can't you do anything to heal your own pain?" he asked.

Our usual conversation was an amicable bickering. He was a convinced conventional doctor and I a healer, forever searching for a deeper understanding of what I was doing. I fascinated him in our shared desire to help the suffering, but at the same time it irritated him when I held my ground in our discussions. Above all, he was curious how I—an otherwise intelligent person—could be so naïve as to believe all this non-scientific stuff like faith healing and homeopathy.

He: "Homeopathy is nothing but superstition. Tiny sugar balls, filled with air! They can never work."

I: "The so-called 'air' in them contains the finer energies of natural elements, which are lost in the chemical processing of these substances in allopathic medication."

Max: "See what I mean? There is not a single molecule to be found of the original curative substance."

I: "I am talking about, for instance, the light-element of the plants, or their connection with the mineral life inside the earth—with life itself, really! Homeopathy does not see illness as an isolated incidence, and its medication works at balancing disharmony in body, mind and soul to assist our innate healing power."

He: "I think it is an air bubble in the mind, not all that much different from the African witchdoctors who, with stones and bones, chase out the spirits that presumably cause an illness."

I: "They use prayer too, like I do!"

Today he saw that I was in pain and he was mellow and compassionate.

"You always lay your hands on other people's pain; why don't you do the same for yourself?" he asked.

I sighed. "You know, 'healer heal thyself' is the hardest assignment for us healers."

"Why is that?"

Tiredly, I uttered the sad truth: "I do try, but it doesn't work because my heart cannot believe that it works for me too."

He looked amazed, and I added:

"I feel love for the people who come and ask for my help. It is easy to believe that God loves them as well and is willing to heal them, but so hard to trust that he loves me enough to do the same for me."

"But how is that possible?" he exclaimed.

"It is a small step from my love to God's love for others," I said. "But I guess it means that I do not love myself a whole lot."

"You are a believing Christian; then how can you not believe that your God loves you? And you have so many people around you who love you, why can't you love yourself?"

I looked him in the eyes and asked: "Do you love yourself?"

"Well, yes, I guess.... I never thought about it, really," he answered thoughtfully. "I don't think I have a problem."

"So many people struggle with this issue," I said. "I can try to explain it, if you have time?"

"Yes, I do," he answered. "Everything is ready. We have set up our tent, Marlene is having a nap and the children are gathering firewood for the cooking. I can sit with you for a while."

"I am learning to love myself and believe that God loves me," I began a difficult explanation, "but at times the road is as rough as the one we just traveled on."

After an emotionally difficult childhood, I had done psychotherapy for many years, and I was aware that the past was the greatest obstacle to the peace of God I was yearning for.

"Many of us carry hurts from the time we were trusting, defenseless children, old pains buried deep within," I said. "They form a programming, which makes us respond with unexplained fear, anger, or guilt feelings to any situation that triggers it.

"We need a safe world to grow up in. Natural disasters like floods and earthquakes destroy the basic trust in the planet as a safe home."

"Of course," Max said. "And in my work I see how extreme poverty teaches a young child that the meaning of life is to survive by any possible means. It definitely blocks the trust that is the condition for a creative approach to life."

"Do you remember a lot about the Second World War?" I asked him.

"No, I was born immediately after," he answered. "But I grew up with the stories, of course."

"Yes, the time hope revived! Well, war conditions us to a gut feeling that life is about being continuously threatened, together with the society to which we belong. Our back may always stay tense and our shoulders never relax because, subconsciously, we are permanently ready to flee."

"Do you think these memories still bother you?" he asked.

"It is long ago, of course," I said. "I was born two months before the Germans invaded The Netherlands. Still, the fear of the bombers flying over still remains etched in me. In Nairobi, the student pilots fly over our house, and whenever they stall the engine in mid-air, I become rigid. This was the fearful reaction of my parents to that sound. It meant that the plane, which probably was carrying bombs, was in trouble and might fall on our house and kill us.

"Emotionally this may keep us permanently prepared for attack; mentally we base our decisions on the fear that death may fall out of the sky at any moment, and spiritually we don't know where we stand with humans capable of doing this to fellow humans. And all this is buried so deeply in our subconscious that we are not aware of it."

The sound of wild flapping and splashing interrupted me as a couple of pelicans landed on the water close to where we were sitting. They performed their landing with an ease as if their huge bodies and beaks were feather-light and, within a few seconds, these amazing creatures, which have a wingspan up to three meters and weigh between five and eight kilos, were sliding stately over the water.

"We need a safe home," I continued my line of thought. "When parents divorce, the basic unity they represent is broken up and, emotionally, this tears a child apart. However strong the reassurances of eternal love, it will feel rejected by the parent who leaves. Later in life, this may result in a subconscious fear of being rejected by a loved one, and then the adult will respond with fear, anger, or grief whenever the old programming perceives a situation to be similar.

"Divorce of the parents is a deep blow to a child's basic trust in love as wholeness, and to the meaning of love as unconditional belonging together, of feeling at one with the rest of mankind," I concluded passionately.

Our children were playing in the distance, happy and carefree in the love of their parents for them and for each other. We watched them, absorbed in a world of their own, gathering around something lying at the muddy shore where the shallow water was smelly with sulfur and bird droppings. At their approach, the thick rows of flamingos had moved away in a single movement, like a pink wave.

"It looks like they found something," I said.

"Maybe it is a dead flamingo, ripped apart and eaten by the fish eagles," Max said. "Soon we will see them coming with a collection of feathers,"

"The flamingo feathers are so spectacular," I said, "white and dark brown, and then pink ranging from the most delicate light to deep dark. I'm always dreaming of using them in a painting, like a collage or so."

"Luckily the smell goes after a while," Max said. "But carry on, I know your own parents were divorced."

"My father left us when I was eight years old. A father stands for the first and most important male person in our life. And so, in the one-sided truth of my perception as a child, a father became someone who is never there when the pain of life becomes too much; who loves us as much as we love him, but at the same time conveys the unspoken message: 'I love you, but you are not worth staying home for.'

"This created a blueprint for profound unhappiness. After a series of crises later in life, I finally understood that I did not know how to trust love and that I needed professional help.

"In psychotherapy, I have worked my way through deeper and deeper layers of grief, anger, fear, and guilt feelings, reliving every hurt until its memory lost its power."

"What a painful process," Max said.

"Yes, but it was worth it, because in the end I came to realize that the whole problem was a signpost of an underlying existential problem: 'God does not love me. I cannot love the Father-Creator enough to keep him close. And even if he loves me, this does not mean that he is there for me whenever I cannot cope with life.' My human father brought home to me that this was what needed to be faced and solved for once and for all."

"Did this part of the process take you long?" he asked.

"Yes, years. Mending trust in love and learning to love myself is still going on; otherwise I would be able to heal myself, wouldn't I?

"Still, God was present when I was young. I am born in a long lineage of church ministers, and I was privileged to grow up in a family that lived with God, all of us in our own confused way. The only one who was not confused was my brother Han, who had Down's syndrome. He was the sweetest, most loving being and his faith was a rock on which we all seemed to lean."

"Yes," Max said, "I love them. Their innocence is so endearing."

"He loved people and he was always trying to bring them together. This desire had its roots in his faith. God was his heavenly Father and dear Lord Jesus, the Good Shepherd, his role model. He was forever gathering people, reconciling them, and trying to mend what was broken. He had his little hands full with my mother and me, forever fighting! When he was fifty-five years old, he died of Alzheimer's disease, but he is forever a most precious memory in my heart."

I was quiet for a moment, remembering his unhappiness, but also the impact his love had had on others. He had been the reason for my questioning of 'why?' from an early age on. I loved him so much that I refused to accept as a coincidence the fact that I could evolve my mind and my life in a normal way, while he could not and suffered for it.

"Do you think you found an answer?" Max asked gently.

"I do. He evolved his heart instead of his mind, and until the very end, he was a great inspiration to others."

Max was moved. "So he was the one who inspired you to go to your heart, where the mind could not bring you peace?"

Costyn came running, in high spirits and excited. "Mummy, we are going up to the pool to swim. Are you coming?"

"No darling, I'm lazy, I'll stay here."

"Okay," he replied and ran back to the other children.

My own son. "I often feel the deepest gratitude for the wonderful mind of my child and the way he is growing up to a full life. For so long I have experienced how different it can be."

I sighed, and then shook it all off again.

"In my mid-twenties, I broke off my relationship with God the Father. I decided that he was asleep or busy elsewhere and that I was better off on my own."

"Quite frankly, that is how I feel, with all the misery I meet in my work," Max interrupted.

"I understand," I replied. "However, God has his own ways of pulling us to the truth, and my path has taken me beyond that feeling.

"Exploring the town in our early days in Kenya, I happened to walk into the Raja Yoga center of the Brahma Kumaris—the Sisters of Brahma. The founder of this Indian order of God-loving sisters for them has been an incarnation of Lord Brahma, the Creator. They envision a world of peace and purity, and their mission is to help people to become aware of the divine Flame within.

"It seemed interesting to hear about their religion and I enrolled in the free course they offered."

"What made you do that?" Max asked. "Were you interested in Hindu philosophy before?"

"No," I replied. "I was just curious, or so I thought."

"Did you find anything there?" he asked.

"I did. Apart from their doctrines, they taught meditation, and for the first time in my life I meditated."

"Lately, when I am in Nairobi for a weekend, our friend Klaas and I follow a course in meditation," Max came in. "At least we try, but as soon as we are back in the car we explode in laughter. All this quasi-scientific talk they dish up in explanation of what it does to even your body. This is just too much for two doctors!"

Max was rather small, but Klaas was a big hulk of a man whose car hardly fitted around him. He had a booming voice and I could well imagine them roaring together.

"Maybe the meditation is freeing you up then!" I laughed. "I know the one you are trying is rather commercial, but I assure you that meditation can be experienced in a very constructive way.

"Indians have an age-old tradition of meditation. It is somehow easier for them to sink into the silence within and find a way back to the spark of God, which they know within us all."

"What is the difference between prayer and meditation?" Max asked.

"I see prayer as talking to God and meditation as listening. Inner silence enables us to listen to answers that we do not hear when we talk. But both reach outside the mind that goes round and round in the circles of fear, confusion, and often senseless chatter.

"Meditation an best be start with controlled breathing in order to relax the body—which would not be a bad idea at the beginning of prayer either! While it concentrates on breathing, the restless mind cannot think. And as it calms down, we begin to experience how it feels to be at peace—the same peace we may experience after we have finished actively talking to God. Both are an expression of the desire to communicate with the Highest, to open up and connect to divine compassion that is love and life."

"Do you consider what you call the Highest to live within us?" he asked.

"What else can I understand if that is where I communicate?

"Anyway, it was during a meditation in the pure energy of devotion of the sisters that I realized how I was projecting on God the complicated mixture of pain, fear, guilt and love, which the concept of 'father' meant to me. Safe in the love of sweet Sister Joshi, my resistance broke down. And as I let my tears flow, God gave me a vision.

"I saw a huge arm in a white sleeve with the mighty hand of God reaching out to me. Fathers hurt, so I was too scared to go forward and take it. Then Costyn, who had just turned four, appeared. He took me by the hand, pulled me forward without hesitation, and he said: 'Come on Mummy, I'll take you there!" And over the years he did, with his unconditional trust in God and with the help of many loving others.'

Max smiled. "That is beautiful. Why do you call it a vision? Was it not a fantasy?"

"I don't think so," I said. "It was so clear and real and profound. And even if it was a fantasy, it was comforting and healing."

"In what way?" he asked.

"Costyn's unconditional trust in God and his love for me showed me the way out of fear, the fear of love."

"Are you still going to the Sisters?" Max asked.

"No, I love and respect their devotion and their work, but the peace I found with them took me back to my love for Jesus, my home. Even during the time I did not want to have anything to do with the Father, Jesus always stayed close to my heart. To deny him would have been denying myself."

Max asked: "These pictures you have in your house of an Indian man with bushy hair in an orange robe, who is he?"

"He is Sathya Sai Baba, the Indian spiritual leader of mankind. Like Jesus, he teaches that we are all brothers and sisters, whatever may be our race, status in life, or religion and that our heart and our mind are the holy home of God."

"What is his religion called?"

"He does not offer us a new religion; all religions come to him. He wants us to be excellent in our own religion, because that is our path in life. He does not convert anyone to anything, except to the heart, but he has specific teachings on how to get there, of course. As for me, I feel like he grabbed me by the neck and said,

"'Do you want to know your Jesus? I'll teach you.' And he did!"

Pieter came to bring us coffee, and he pulled up a chair. I told him that I was trying to explain Sai Baba.

"How can you love an Indian holy man while you are a Christian?" Max asked.

"I see Baba and Jesus each as a different expression of perfect divine love. So are we, of course, but our consciousness is limited and theirs is not. You can read in the Bible how Jesus knew the inner feelings and thoughts of everyone. So does Baba. But above all, the difference with us is that all sorts of conditions limit our love, where theirs is unconditional and limitless. Of course, it took time for me to understand this. When I first heard about him, I felt in my heart that I knew him but I was so confused. He heals the sick and raises the dead. He teaches God's love and he loves humanity in the same way as Jesus did—and still does! He manifests God on earth, but how could there be anyone living today the same as Jesus?

"He gently reassured me that I could love both him and Jesus. That it is the human mind that puts labels on ideas, while the divine Mind is all-encompassing. Jesus said: 'I have come for the whole world,' which made many people around Him very cross, by the way. They wanted to be exclusive. Like Jesus, Baba is inclusive. He is here for all."

"Do you mean that both have the same function for us?"

"We all need the same medicine, don't we, only the dosage varies? Baba teaches us how to pull forth the love of the heart from under the cement blocks of mind constructions, to uncover the divine essence of man beneath the layers of fear, guilt, anger, and grief.

"His lesson is compassion and he makes everyone work as he says: 'Hands that help are holier than lips that pray'.

It is his mission to bring mankind to realize that there is but one religion: the religion of love; only one language: the language of the heart, and the one Self, which God created, expressed in every single one of us. And each religion is to be respected as a path back to that realization."

"I still don't understand why you need a guru when you have your Jesus," Max declared.

"Well, you know, when I am confused and unhappy, in my head I may well know that Jesus is with me in Spirit, but by the nature of my state of mind and emotions, I am blocked to him. I cannot sense his loving presence. Because of his human manifestation, I can always relate to Baba, though. There are books, tapes, pictures and even airline tickets to Puttaparthi in South India where he lives. We can talk about him with each other, think of him day and night and replace our unhappy thoughts with the holiness of God.

"Baba says: 'To see your own eyes, you need a mirror; to see yourself in your native grandeur, you need a guru (preceptor).' In my yearning for my hidden inner grandeur, I have always projected on Jesus the dream of what I wanted to become. Baba inspires me as the present day physical manifestation of that dream on earth. As we imbue Baba with the deepest Self we yearn to bring out, in all he is and does he reflects back to us who we are."

"Now I don't have a clue what you are talking about," Max burst out, slightly irritated.

"May I tell you another vision I was given, as an example of what is happening to me?"

"Go ahead," he answered

"We had come together in the sitting room of an Indian family to sing bahjans, devotional songs, that are mainly sung in Sanskrit. On these occasions, Indians always sit cross-legged on the hard floor and I was very uncomfortable in my pain.

"Singing with my eyes closed, I began to forget my body, and then an unexpected scene unfolded before my inner eye.

"I saw how Baba came to stand in the doorway. I fell on my knees. I bowed down at his feet and touched the ground with my forehead in reverence. In my heart I exclaimed, 'Lord, into all eternity I don't want to be anywhere else! This is where I want to stay forever.'

Gently mocking me, Baba smiled: 'If you don't mind, I'll go and do something else in the meantime,' and moved on.

I cried: 'Stop Swami, I'm coming with you!'

"I left my body where it was and, together with its pain, I left behind the belief in time and space. I expanded into the cosmos, one with him and free of all limitations. I can assure you that it was bliss to experience my expanded self and to be away from the body and its weight of pain."

"I can imagine," Max said while he gently touched my back.

"When I looked down, I saw my body change into a mountain of sweet scented frangipani flowers, velvety white with yellow hearts—a sign that one day my physical existence on earth will be light, delicate in strength and unbroken as God created it?"

"I do hope so for you," Max said warmly.

"Sai Baba came into my life to be my father for as long as I needed one. Infinite love can absorb all projections and he answered mine with love. He filled my life with miracles and, ever so gently, he coaxed me back to trust. Holding on to the orange robes of the Father, over time the emotional pain slowly poured out of me in endless tears, and within myself I became reconciled with my physical father—who had long died—and with the Creator God.

Pieter knew the story and he sat quietly looking over the water. When I had come to my conclusion, he remarked,

"Look! There is something amazing going on with the flamingos."

Flamingos spend the greater part of their lives with their slender necks bent down into the water. They are equipped with an angled bill, which allows their head to stay horizontal while, clacking and slobbering, they filter the alkaline water for algae all day long.

Now however, with their heads lifted up, they were involved in a rhythmic stepping forward and backward. After a while, we discovered a distinct pattern in their movement. First they took some steps forward, then came to a short halt, dipped their heads gracefully in the water and, again in a rhythmic movement, a couple of times lifted their necks high up. Each one then finished his or her part in the movement by stepping back and allowing others to take their place. Another group did the opposite at the other side of an imaginary line. They seemed to dance in a mirror image.

In disciplined rows of two by two, long lines of always more birds came from further down the lake, swimming, stepping on the water, and even flying in well-disciplined V-formations, and joined the others without disrupting the dance.

Awed by the perfect harmony of the moving and arriving birds, we watched them for a long time and tried to figure out what made them perform this dance.

Suddenly Pieter broke the fascinated silence and said,

"You know what? There is a sweet-water outlet here from the stream that comes down from the spring higher up among the fig trees. They are drinking fresh water!"

Wistfully he added, "If only humans could live in this disciplined harmony, especially sharing clean drinking water."

Meanwhile, my thoughts had drifted home, where I had to lie down so often. Four years earlier, normal life as I had known it, had come to a halt when I needed an operation on my back. This had only solved part of the problem and often I was forced to rest for weeks on end.

I spent many hours staring at the big wild fig tree with its busy bird life and soaking up the healing beauty of the colors in the garden in the brilliance of the equatorial light. Isolated from most of normal society and often desperate and lonely, my search for God could not but intensify. And in the silence of my loneliness, I learned to listen to the inner voice, the still voice of the heart that bears all wisdom in heaven and on earth, your voice, mine, the voice for God.

"We have forgotten to base our decisions in life on the wisdom of the whisperings of our heart," I went on. "And so often we have suppressed with our mind what our heart told us would make us happy, that our body breaks up under the relentless stress.

"Illness then is a cry from the depth of our being that the fear to surrender to the inspirations of our heart needs to be healed. It has to make room for other aspects in us to grow and expand. When we fall ill, something in us is ready for a new stage in life. The time has come to make a new choice and we withdraw from the scene."

"Do you see even your own back problem as a result of suppressed fears, then?" Max asked.

"Yes, too many old memories that are 'proof' that God does not love me, remember?"

"Healing can begin when we face and accept the fact that memories belong to the past and nowhere else. At present, there is no plane flying over my head, preparing to drop a bomb on me while I have never done anything to harm the pilot. And so I can let go of this fear and its manifestations. There is no one in this group of friends, least of all Pieter or Costyn, who will attack me verbally or emotionally, nor will they leave me as my father did, so I can stop hiding behind the fences of my heart. The past can go with the bombers and the memories can follow them on the scrap heap.

"The road is often long and painful, but the reward is glorious. When we arrive at the bottom of the pit of our darkest emotions, we have nowhere else to go but up to where the light is. We look up, or deep within, which is the same, and the light that is the truth of our being, God, gradually begins to reveal itself. We find Spirit, who has been there all along, loving us and allowing us to find our way back to our essence in our own sweet time. This is why an illness needs to be prolonged, at times. Time creates the opportunity for the process to evolve and settle within us on all levels."

"But how do you connect all this to your healing power?" Max asked.

"Underneath the rubble of bad memories, of fear, grief, anger, or even hatred, sparkles a gem of love. Fear keeps the body shackled, but love is harmony that transforms into health. If the sufferer can be brought to accept love to counterbalance fear, anxiety changes into peace. A balanced mind and heart can then draw upon the innate restorative power of the physical body. This is why it is called spiritual healing. Love always works."

"Do you feel it will work for you too, then?" Max asked.

"Gradually, yes, I think so. At least now it has given me the strength to come along on safari instead of staying home and being more comfortable, but so lonely and alone with my pain."

Max turned to Pieter and asked, "What do you think of all this; you work with scientific methods and precision instruments. Do you believe in spiritual healing?"

"I don't understand what she does," Pieter answered, "but I respect it because I see how people change."

This aroused Max' interest. "What do you see then?"

"Often people arrive all stressed out with fear or pain," Pieter said, "but when they leave, their faces are so different, relaxed, with color in their cheeks and peace in their eyes."

Max looked at me, "Then what is it you do? How do you do it?"

"I administer love! When I lay my hands on places in the body where the pain or the disease is located, I become very quiet within. Great warmth enters me, to flow out again through my hands, which feel hot and tingling. It flows into the other person and makes him or her relax deeply. The pain goes and often the problem gets cured altogether. It is love that flows through me into the suffering other. And it works not only on a physical problem, but for a suffering mind and emotions, too."

"Tell me about this distance healing people talk about. After all you have told me, I feel I can no longer say that it is all just nonsense, but what can you do when you do not have your patient within arm's reach?"

"Mentally I put myself in the same position. I go to the inner source, but instead of the warmth flowing from my hands, it flows out from my heart area."

"Do you really think this reaches the other?" Max asked, a little incredulously.

"There are several stories in the Bible of distant healing Jesus performed. Do you know the story of Jesus and the Roman officer? This man politely sent some Jewish elders to ask Jesus to heal his servant. Jesus agreed and went on his way to the officer's house, but before long, a message from the officer reached him that he did not have to come all the way. It would be enough if he just spoke the word, and the illness would go. Jesus praised the officer's faith and the servant was healed at that instant."

"It only works if the other person also believes in God, of course," Max concluded, "preferably the same God."

"That helps, but it is not a condition, as long as the healer has faith in love," I answered. "Still, there has to be someone, even another person, who asks for the healing—out of love. All love is healing."

"Your secret is love then," he smiled.

"Yes. And this love I call God."

"I have seen you with Gerald the other day. He was in dreadful pain and he could not move his neck; it was as stiff as a piece of wood. For five days, I had been treating him with medication but in half an hour you had him up and about to celebrate New Years Eve! I was too perplexed to ask you about it."

"That was my first public healing," I laughed, "from then on, everyone knew."

"Why can't everybody do it?" he asked.

"Everyone can administer love, straight from one heart to the other, like a mother kisses away the pain of her child."

"And now something else. How do you see the difference between psychotherapy and spiritual healing?" Max asked.

"It is my own experience that psychotherapy uses the mind and the emotions and also the resistance in the body, these days, to break through to the original causes of emotional distress. The aim is for the client to experience that the source of the pain is in the past and has nothing to do with the present. In spiritual healing love short-circuits those and goes straight to the heart and its yearning for love, its incapacity to give or receive it, or both."

"There is one thing I never understand," Pieter said. "I often see you in a lot of pain, but as soon as you feel better, people come for help. How can you help others if you are not healed yourself?"

"Maybe the truth I search for lies in the other," I answered. Some time ago I asked Jesus the same question, 'Jesus, how can I help to heal others if I believe in my own pain, which is not your truth, nor an expression of your love?'

"Jesus answered me, 'To give is to receive.' He meant that to give love through my hands or otherwise, helps me to realize that love is the very essence of my being. My own healing will gradually come from sharing love."

"You know very well what you are doing, don't you?" Max said with a grin.

"Now you see why you may consider taking us seriously," I laughed, "and why healers are not the competition to conventional medicine, but its complement. Side by side with the doctor, like priests of the Most High, we administer forgiveness and love. A doctor, too, is a priest in his own right."

I just loved the amazed look on his face and, delighted, I explained my vision.

"Yes doctor, you hear me right! Regardless of whether you are religious in the conventional meaning of the word or not, whenever you bring us back to normal with your knowledge and your care, you are an emissary of the Creator who created us whole and healthy. Like a priest, you proclaim that the past is forgiven and healed and can be released."

"I must admit that this is not quite my day to day philosophy," he said, "but I am happy with your view. Of course there is a deep truth about our profession, but I have never seen it that way."

"I call Spirit love, and in you Spirit works as your medical knowledge, your devotion to your profession, and your compassion for your patients."

"You call both my mind and my feelings Spirit?"

"Spirit must be their origin. They are not material, are they?

"We may call Spirit God, Yahweh, Allah, Shiva, Vishnu, Jesus, Buddha, or Sai Baba. It is the all-present Divine, pervading and transcending us. It is what we all are, nobody excluded, where the priest or priestess is one with the person who is seemingly beyond rescue, buried in a grave of fear, anger, guilt and pain. This is where the healthy meets the sick in the compassion, which has its origin in the sense of unity among us all. We answer the call for belonging. Don't you find yourself putting a reassuring hand on a patient's arm at times?"

"Of course," he said. "It is an impulse to share, to show that I understand."

"As compassion, Spirit in me can always reach out to Spirit in you, even without words. Whatever the appearances, it knows the most inner you as whole and perfect, in peace, and loved forever and ever as God created you."

Inspired I continued, "When Spirit in me touches Spirit in you, it strengthens the remembrance of who you truly are.

"Spirit, expressing itself as my life, can touch yours. When you are too confused, or in pain, or too scared to recognize who you are, the divine 'I' in me, which I share with you but which you cannot reach, can heal you. The medicine I administer is love and love is life. That is how Jesus raised the dead."

"The other day, I overheard Costyn explain what you are doing," Pieter said. "You know what he said? 'My mother helps people to heal themselves.' As little as he is, he knows!"

After a while I continued, "Whether recovery is instantaneous or slow depends on a readiness to accept healing that is beyond our conscious control. Like you, we can never promise others healing on the physical level, even though this often happens. The heart may need more time to heal and learn to trust again. Timing is between the sufferer and God, but I always promise peace.

"'Peace I give you, my peace I leave you,' Jesus said and that is the peace I may convey, because it is mine as my deepest truth."

"And your prescription is love," Max concluded.

Later in the evening, we were all gathered around the campfire. The air was warm, the sky was dark and the moon was full. As it reflected on the water, it drew a wide silver path of light.

"You see," I said, "the moon reflects the sunlight, the water mirrors the moon, and we reflect God, the Source of all creation."

The flamingos were still awake and active. Every once in a while, a couple of them flew up from the water and then another dance began. Borne on the thermal of the lake, they circled higher and higher until they seemed to be no more than dark silhouettes, near to touching the moon.

"Paradise, a wing-beat away," Pieter mused.

Paradise lost

Then life collapsed around us. We lost everything to a crooked business partner and the corruption in the country. And there was nothing we could do. In a country where justice goes to the highest bidder, there is no point in taking someone to court when you do not have any money. Even our savings were gone and we were left with one month's rent for the house.

With his company, Pieter had sent crews into the field with vehicles, well equipped with instruments to survey the water situation deep down in the earth. It was the realization of his dream to provide the poor and neglected with the water of life and he had built it up over ten years. Now he suffered the heartbreak of losing it. No one could rob him of his excellent reputation of professional knowledge, however, and experience, and work kept coming his way. From deep within, he pulled the strength to carry on, on his own.

Costyn had finished school. Before he would start university, he wanted a year off to do something else, so luckily we did not have to pay for further studies in The Netherlands, yet. God gave him work to do that he thoroughly enjoyed and he stayed on in Nairobi to support us with his calm inner light.

A few months after all this happened, circumstances called me to my own country for two months. The Netherlands consist of all but forty one thousand square kilometers, on which we live with 16 million people. There is an extensive and complicated bureaucratic system to make it work and it is efficient but cumbersome. In Kenya, bureaucracy mainly serves to create more chaos, and every law provides an opportunity for corruption and extortion.

When I came back home from Holland to the contrast of Kenya, I felt sick and tired of the inertia of the state, the immorality of anyone with power over anyone else, the inefficiency, and the problems that were not mine. Pieter was away most of the time, Costyn would soon be leaving for good, and the loneliness in the big empty house on the hilltop would only get worse. Why would I continue to put so much energy and time in managing the large house, six acres of garden, and six staff, mostly for myself alone?

Divine love offered Pieter a well-paid contract for a year and a half in Botswana, in Southern Africa. Now the big question was: what to do with the house? Pieter had been so happy in the sacred haven in which he had manifested his dream and where he always returned to peace from the difficult world outside, and to the love of people, animals, and flowers. He was not ready to let it go, but would it make sense to continue to pay the rent and all the staff, while we could only be there during the holidays? Obviously not, seeing our financial situation. A good compromise seemed to be to try and find someone who would take it from us for that period.

The only reason why I was willing to hang on to the house was the garden I had created. Often I sat in the colorful inner courtyard, surrounded by the dogs, with cats peeping from corners and gutters and monkeys chasing each other over the roofs, and thinking how most of humanity would be delighted with nothing more than this small garden alone. Who needs six acres more to cultivate, plus another five of jungle, with all the work it takes?

We found a young family who were willing to take over the house until our return to Kenya. It seemed perfect that they would keep the staff and take care of the animals; the cars could stay parked in the compound, and they were happy to use quite a bit of the furniture, which then would not have to be put in storage.

I began to prepare the house for moving and storing. The major players in the game could not help me. They were gone. Pieter had already left to start his job in Botswana and Costyn was in The Netherlands. And so divine Presence had to do the job with me. It did. Even from where I least expected it, it manifested everyone I needed to fulfill a task that was way too heavy for me with my damaged back. And I accepted all the help with gratitude.

I arranged, cleared out, and threw away. Stuff had to go to Botswana; stuff stayed in the house. Stuff was to be stored, and I put stickers on everything: red on what was going to be sent to Botswana and green on the storage material. I had to take a decision about every single thing until I got sick and tired of 'stuff'. The whole exercise was a tremendous lesson in decision taking.

I had made arrangements with a removal company, and four days before I was to leave, early in the morning the movers arrived. Soon people were wrapping and packing all over the sprawling house, while I dashed back and forth to check on all and everyone. When the heavy truck finally left with its load by the end of the afternoon, the noise and the chaos went with it, and a sudden silence fell.

The golden late afternoon light was glowing as beautifully as ever, but I looked around at the cracks in floors and walls that were now mercilessly exposed, and I thought: "Do I really have to come back to this 'rubbish house' as the contractor had called it ten years ago? With all the work it takes, and never enough light coming in through the cute little windows to show off my paintings?"

I had not heard from the people who were coming to live in the house, for a while, and we still had to finalize the details, so I called. The lady answered the phone. In a timid, hesitant voice she said:

"Ah well, you know, my husband does not want us to live there after all. He is working outside the country a lot and he says it is not a safe place."

I was speechless, so she continued: "It is too far out as well; my children's friends live at the other side of the town. And anyway the period we can have it is too short."

Finally I managed to bring out:

"Did you really have to wait this long before telling me?" and I slammed down the receiver.

I was shocked, but at the same time a feeling of relief surged through me. God seemed to be giving me my heart's desire of releasing what was becoming a burden. For my family's sake, I had tried to hold on to the house and I had failed. Now I could do the one thing I really wanted: clear out the whole place and give it back to the landlord. It had been paradise, but life changes and evolves, and its needs with it.

I wanted to join Pieter so badly but, of course, I now had to postpone my departure. And this is where the real hard work began.

Apart from the six rondavels, there were several outbuildings, plus two guesthouses, and what was left of the workshop after the mechanics had moved to another location. Every nook and corner was crammed with ten years of stuff one does not throw away in a third world country, because it may always be of some use.

I also had to help my staff to find new jobs. This is the best way to provide for their future. Prospective employers like to get personal recommendations; and without telephone or often even a post box, it is very hard for the poor to find new employment on their own.

I also had to find good homes for all the animals. This was not going to be easy for most people are only interested in puppies and kittens, not in older animals. Some of the remaining furniture could also go in storage, but the rest I had to sell. This included Pieter's vintage MG and my beautiful twenty-year old Volvo, the camper, a sailing boat and my antique small grand piano. This lovely instrument had been brought into Kenya by a British noble lady in the beginning of 1900, and must have traveled on a steam train from the seaport Mombassa to Nairobi.

A lot of our things were old and worn. My heart wanted nothing better than to give everything away, apart from the valuables, and leave as quickly as possible to be with Pieter. But I told myself that we needed the money, since we had to start a new household, and so I did what everybody does—I tried to sell just about everything that was not falling apart. This meant advertising, getting countless phone calls, receiving people, and at times even driving around to deliver.

Long before I had finished, I became exhausted to the point of collapse and I went for help to a Chinese doctor whom I had seen in the past. He and his caring nurses kept me going with massage, acupuncture and herbal concoctions, but at the end of a week most of the money I had earned with selling 'stuff' had moved into his pocket. I sometimes wondered how much more insane I could get, but I did not know how to stop—obsessed as I was with our financial problems and my hurry to leave.

I managed to empty the whole place in three weeks, and all the while my heart was so heavy. It was farewell to the place where our child had grown up, where we had been happy with an abundance of houseguests and visitors, with the Africans who lived with us, and with our animals and flowers. Here Pieter had materialized and lived his dream and I had worked through ten years of my incapacitating back problem. In this magical place, which had been like a temple, the physical pain had made me withdraw deep within myself, to be the tool of my inner transformation.

It hurt so much to give away our darling animals and part with my team of faithful helpers, with whom we had shared our lives as with close relatives.

Divine love, knowing what was ahead of me, sent me Lia. She was an ordained minister, a modest and loving person who had evolved into a spiritual healer and a clairvoyant. Both of us had our beloved Jesus in the center of our life.

She came over for lunch one day and I showed her the house, which, even though half empty, was still amazing. Then we went out into the garden and we walked slowly around, while Lia took in the power of the ancient holy place, very concentrated within herself. Silently she communicated with nature.

Suddenly she bent down to an aloe flower in the rock garden. It had been raining heavily and, dripping water, its head drooped low to the ground. Ever so gently she caressed it and she said: "It is weeping because you are going. All weep because you leave."

She looked at me and, surprisingly, she added, "You are fragile, so fragile."

She made a butterfly movement with her hands. "You are ready to take off."

"Fragile? I?" I exclaimed, "I am strong. Look what I am doing here all by myself. All I need is a good rest!"

Gardener Jonathan walked by. He smiled at us. I loved him. He was a beautiful, gentle being and I sensed in him a very old soul with a long history on the planet. In my heart I knew that, this time, God had allowed him to incarnate in the limited existence of a rural African, poor but with a strong connection to the ancient values. In a simple life of working with plants and the earth and with no more demands than being able to provide for his loved ones, he walked close to Jesus and the Father.

Lia agreed when I told her this and she said,

"His young body can hardly bear his old soul. He is a very good person. You can always trust him."

"I know," I replied.

My friends got very worried about me being all by myself in that lonely place at night. I did not see the problem, and I assured them that I was fine. The gardeners were living in the compound and the watchmen protected me at night. I was safe. In the evenings, I made a roaring fire, pulled the old sofa close and, surrounded by the cats and the dogs and with the parrot babbling on my shoulder, I was happy. Curled up in bed, later, I was contented with my last nights in the cozy round bedroom. It was my way of taking leave of the house and our life as it had been.

Then, one evening I suddenly felt agitated. Anxiety about new jobs for the people, homes for the animals— who would want a cat with a litter, or a fourteen-year-old tomcat—and the thousand things I still had to do, all kept spinning in my mind and I could not sleep. The time seemed to have come to get out of the house in the evenings and spend the last nights with friends.

Close to my heart was a young South-Indian family. They were like my own, my children, their beautiful little daughter my grandchild. The next morning I gave Bhuvaneswari a call:

"I'm going crazy here. Let me come and stay with you tonight."

"Yes. And come early. I'll cook you a nice dinner," she said warmly.

Mmm...,the thought of her delicious Southern Indian food was enough to keep me going through my day.

It was Tamil New Year's Eve.

Traditionally Indians live together as an extended family; the oldest son always stays with the parents, even when he marries and, together with his wife, takes care of them till the end of their days. On New Year's Day, at four in the morning everyone has already bathed and dressed in new clothes to begin the day with prayers. Also, in a special ceremony in front of the Gods, the mother of the household is honored with the gift of a new sari. Their own mothers were far away in India, but to my delight 'my children' presented me with a beautiful gold colored one.

In all the hardship of what I had to go through on my own, God never ceased to shower me with the blessings of his Presence. Divine love not only manifested people to help me to do what was necessary, but also graced me with 'extras', like new friendships from people who originally had only come to buy, and now the generous gift of this beautiful sari!

The evening was going to be spent in the temple and so, when I came back from my day's work, Bhuvaneswari lovingly wrapped the golden sari around me in the complex traditional Tamil way. With her sweet face and her heavy black hair, she too looked gorgeous in a new sari. Ramanan, her handsome husband, was dashing, dressed in white, and elf-like little Amrutha seemed to have walked straight out of a fairytale book in her sparkling dress. Together we left for the temple, and singing and praying to the Gods and the Goddesses, we spent our evening in devotion.

And that was the end of peace.

The next morning I got a call from my housekeeper, Rose. The house had been broken into and the safe was stolen. My passport, money, documents and antique jewelry were all gone. David, Jonathan's colleague was gone too, as well as the one watchman who had been with us for years.

David knew the house inside out. He had always repaired the walls and the ceilings and done the occasional painting. In the most vulnerable place of the house, the backroom of my studio, he had broken the window and cut the grills with our own tools. The big axe was gone as well.

Rose cried and Jonathan was trembling with shock and horror—as was I—and they had trouble believing that this had truly happened. For years, they had worked together as a close team and they had never suspected that the two had this dark side in them. They were deeply shaken on my behalf, too. They knew how much we had always helped when they were in need.

Still, it did not take long before I realized how God had protected us. Rose lived with her family in Mwimuto and had gone home in the evening. She had been safe. Jonathan would never be part of such a thing, so they had left him out of their plotting. He had been asleep in the room next to David's, and what had divine Love done but let it rain so hard during the night that he never heard anything! They must have made a racket and if he had woken up and gone out to see what was happening, in the grip of their madness as they were, they would not have hesitated to hurt him badly.

I had been sent away to a safe place. The spinning in my head, which had made me leave the house at night, had been the anger and the plotting I had sensed but not understood, because I was too busy with my 'stuff'.

I was devastated. What could have brought them to do this? We had kept them alive with their families in times of crisis. We had paid doctors, hospital bills, and medication even for their wives and children. During a drought, I had sent the watchman home upcountry with bags of food for his mother and the daughter who had to stay with her to finish school. I had provided the bus fare to bring the rest of his family back to Nairobi, and when they had arrived emaciated, we had given them extra food until they were strong and healthy again.

When I discovered that David was starving because all his money and the extra food I gave him was needed at home, I had a big pot with maize and beans ready every day at midday for all the staff—to be eaten on the spot to make sure they would stay healthy. David's family lived in a poor area of Nairobi—very far from our home—and he had been worried about their safety at night while he was gone to work during the week. We had given him the money for a strong iron door for his house to protect his wife and children. With my husband far away, he had destroyed my protection and robbed me.

Kenya is the first country in Africa where family planning was introduced. Even so, it hardly seemed to have any effect during the twenty years we have lived in Kenya. The population doubled to 30 million people, half of which is below fifteen years of age. This means that too many people have too many children. Even a first world country would have trouble coping with such an amount of young people in need of education and jobs, let alone one ruled by a government that could not care less.

The people who lived with us were doing all right if they had no more than two children. Then they would have enough money to feed and clothe them and, with some extra help from us, get them through their schools and into a profession.

This gardener and watchman had never stopped getting more children, and their problems had increased accordingly. Furthermore, the number of children in their care grew even larger when their brothers and sisters began to die of Aids.

Half a year earlier, David's youngest child, a baby, had been so desperately ill that he and his wife were ready to let her go, but the doctors in the hospital had refused. This also meant that he had to go on paying money, which he did not have, and every two days he kept coming back for more loans. We were having such a hard time ourselves and there were the others to take care of as well. We helped him as much as we could, but there came a moment when I had to refuse.

His response was furious,

"Mama, you have to help me!" in the time-honored African tradition in which the 'haves' share with the 'have-not's'.

Ten days before the robbery, he and I had had the following conversation in the car, on our way to deliver a bed I had sold:

"Mama, do you remember that time when my baby was so sick and you refused to give me more money?"

"Yes, David, you know we couldn't. We did not have it."

"I understand that now, but I was so mad at you. I was even planning bad things," he said, slightly ashamed.

Taking my eyes off the road for a moment, I gave him a surprised look.

"Then one night, I woke up from my sleep because Sai Baba's voice called me," he continued.

"You heard him?"

"Yes. 'What do you think you are doing, David?' he asked me."

Fascinated, I listened with only half an eye on the traffic.

"You actually heard his voice?"

"At first I was so shocked, and then I began to think. I thought of all the things you and Bwana had done for me and I wrote them down. Do you remember that letter I gave you to thank you?"

Of course I did. The way he had carefully listed everything had touched us very much.

He concluded, "I was so grateful that God saved me from what I was planning."

How could I ever, ever have taken this as a warning?

When I told Lia about the robbery, she said that she had sensed fear in the backyard: 'Mama is leaving, who will help us now when we cannot cope with our six children, sickly wife, old parents and the orphans from our brothers and sisters?'

Even though I was in the process of finding them new jobs, they knew that it would take time to build up a relationship with their new employers in which they could ask for extra money in times of crisis. They had turned this fear into the anger they needed to do what they did.

"Let us rob her; she owes us what we steal."

I did not care about the material things I had lost. I was so deeply into the process of detaching and releasing that I actually thought, 'Okay. That means fewer things to take care of.' But it was the 'why' that hurt so badly. The foremost reason why Rose, Jonathan and I were so devastated was that our place had been a temple of God. All of us had been living close to him, each in our own way. We had talked and discussed our views and experiences and, at times, we had prayed together. On Sundays, the Africans spent the whole day in church to celebrate Jesus. During the week they lived with him from the Bible and walked his path. Every Sunday, the watchman sang God's glory in the church choir.

My greatest grief was that the two thieves had lost so much more than I. All I had lost were material goods, but how could they look their Jesus in the eyes from now on?

The gardener had been a faithful father and husband. He loved his family. He had struggled to give them what they needed and now he had become a thief. He had gained some money but lost his self-respect in the eyes of his family who later knew what he had done, his community, and God. As soon as he would come to his senses—and the stolen money was finished—he would realize it.

We had spent together so many hours in making a beautiful garden, and, in one night's work, he had wiped out for himself all the love we had brought into our work. Never again would he be able to think back with joy at what we had created.

Over time, this event made me understand the cosmic impact of our words and deeds, however unimportant or insignificant they may seem.

What had happened appeared to be their evil deed, but I came to realize that I had had my share in it, too. Had I not been so preoccupied with making money with some petty old stuff, I would have caught the signals of fear and then anger brewing in the backyard. If I had listened to my heart, I would have given away everything old and worn, trusting God to provide us with whatever we would need. Then my mind would have been free to pay them attention—to reassure them that change is fearful for everyone, but that God was on our side.

The decision to rob me had been theirs. Mine was the pain of the guilt feelings that fear had made me choose against my heart where paradise is. I had not listened, and thus I had created a space in which they were tempted to spoil their relationship with God and man. It had cost us all dearly.

After two days, we found the safe at the bottom of the garden, cracked open with our own wood axe. Jewelry and money were gone, of course, but they had not bothered about the documents. My passport and air ticket, as well as other papers, had been lying in the rain for thirty hours and were badly damaged and would need to be replaced. People still came to buy and take away the last things and soon, like friends, perfect strangers were helping me to wash the documents and hang them to dry on a string we suspended in the empty kitchen.

After this experience I mistrusted absolutely anyone who came near me, apart from Rose and Jonathan, and that was unbearable.

Broken in body, mind, and heart after yet another sleepless night, I thought,

"I need Lia. Please God, if it is your wish, let her be in her center even though it is Sunday."

Of course she was in when I came.

I collapsed in her arms, crying,

"I am suspicious of everybody. I don't trust anyone anymore. I can't live like this. This is not God's way. I am a healer, for God's sake!"

She held me tight while I cried and cried. Then she took me into one of the rooms and made me lay down on a bed. She covered me with a blanket and lovingly tucked me in. She sat down next to me and she made me talk.

I told her of my love for Jesus, and how I live in his heart and he in mine. How Jesus always had been a tender love in my heart, even during the period in my life when I considered God out, sleeping, and definitely not to be trusted.

"I want to go home so badly," I sobbed. "I want to go Home to my Jesus."

Gently she said: "You can go to him now."

I closed my eyes and I went.

And I saw him. He was waiting for me.

With infinite love in his eyes, he looked at me and he asked,

"Why have you come?"

Standing face to face with him, I answered without hesitating,

"I have not come this far in loving and understanding God in order to leave now. I will stay on earth to help others to get to where I am."

He blessed me, and I brought my consciousness back into my body.

I was quiet for a long time. Finally I opened my eyes and Lia said,

"You have made your choice."

Dazed, I asked, "Did I? Which choice? Now, just now?"

She said, "Yes, you could have chosen to leave the earth soon, and that would have been all right too."

Deeply moved, she added, "You are surrounded by so much love, you are so loved."

I felt nothing but exhaustion and grief, but at least I was calm.

I had been prepared for this moment by Rudolph Steiner, whose lectures on the Gospels I had begun to study when we came to Kenya. Steiner, the founder of Anthroposophy, was seeing and understanding as much in the spiritual world as in the material one. In his books and lectures he explained the connections between the two worlds in detail, and gave a new spiritual foundation to art, medicine, agriculture, education and religion. This experience in our soul's evolution I had just gone through, he calls 'the meeting with the Great Guardian of the Threshold'.

When we have learned all the earth has to teach us, we are free to leave the planet for a life in Spirit. However, together with others we have built our world as it is, with all the misconceptions of what reality means and with all its suffering and hardship, as well as love, joy and creativity. We would not have been able to get through it without others, and so the highest choice is the one of love: stay and help.

There had been none of these considerations in my moment of choice, however. The only thing I felt was,

"I have worked hard to understand what I know now and to love as I do. I want to pass on what I have learned. I want to support others on the path from darkness and confusion into the light and love of God." And this is where the book comes from to you, my dear fellow travelers.

Now life became difficult in a whole new way. I had had the choice to leave, Home had been so close and I found myself still here. I was back in the chaos, the grief and all the complications of our lives. The emotional, mental, and physical exhaustion was still intact and my heart was sick of 'stuff—all these possessions one thinks one needs to drag around the globe and that turn others into thieves.

God knows what he is doing, so whenever I thought,

'I can still change my mind, chose again and go', always my own answer came back to me:

'I have promised to stay and share my Jesus with the world'.

And in the depth of my being, I felt carried by a strength, which I knew was the books waiting to be written for him.

God surrounded me with love. He gave me people to hold me in their arms, comfort me, and make me feel welcome on this earth. With infinite love, over time Jesus and the Father coaxed me back to life on earth.

The last day arrived. Even the house was crying now. There was a heavy rainfall and my art studio was leaking a curtain of water.

Slowly I walked through all the round rooms, filled with the memories of our child growing up, of a fascinating life with people and animals, crystals, paintings and God. I wanted to cleanse and sanctify this temple I was leaving, and dedicate it to the next inhabitants.

For a long time, I had been chanting the Gayatri Mantra. Every morning and evening I had sung this prayer one hundred and eight times until it had become part of me.

Om Bhur Buha Svaha,
Tat Savitur Varenyam
Bhargo Devasya Dheemahi
Dhiyo Yo Nah Prachodayat

Oh Source of all creation,
Creator of all that is,
Light of the World,
Bliss of our Being,
Enlighten our hearts and minds.

These Sanskrit holy words, prayed since time immemorial, are a powerful weapon against every thought that comes up to destroy the peace of God within us. In all my crises, it reminded me that I had to live my earth truth of the moment, that I had to go through the motions, however demanding, but that my basis, my eternal, unalterable truth is God, the Ground of our being.

Embraced by the round walls of our home, I filled each room with the sound of this powerful prayer.

In the dining room I remembered the many who had shared the table with us. The sitting room with the grand piano had been filled with singing and piano music.

In the corridor to Costyn's room, the grief that it was all over forever, became too much to bear. I sank to the floor in tears, while Jonathan, who happened to pass by, looked on helplessly.

Then I went my crystal room, the room where I had spent most of my time of pain, but where I had also sought the truth of God, together with the many who came to share the sacred quest.

Last of all, I came to my prayer room, the tiny round room at the ground floor of the tower. There had been a big double mattress on the floor, the altar a shelf with crystals and a small statue of the Lord Vishnu, pictures of my beloved Jesus and Sai

Baba, and a Buddhist prayer book. Thousands of prayers had been prayed here; it had been filled with tears and ecstasy.

It was empty now and again grief overwhelmed me. Sobbing on the cold, hard floor, I remembered everyone who had passed through this sanctum. It had seen God's love and power at work, both in the visible and the invisible world. It had welcomed the souls of street children, politicians, the corrupt and the righteous.

Angels and nature beings had filled it, invisible helpers of the life forms on the planet, and the Holy Spirit had manifested itself in my visions as Jesus, Sai Baba, the Buddha, and Lord Shiva. I had met the Prophet Mohammed. I had been given to see his beautiful luminous eyes, radiating love when he said to me,

"Now that you have understood that God is One, we can work together."

Often I had experienced merging with Jesus and Sai Baba, teachers of love and anchors of divine compassion on our planet.

In utter amazement, on a rainy Saturday morning, I had sensed myself become a bird with immense wings, Garuda, the bird that carries Lord Vishnu, the preserver of life, the Healer-God with whom I have an ancient bond.

Then, out of the blue, I sensed them come streaming in, my nature beings, the gnomes, the elves and the fairies with whom I had cried, laughed, and created the gardens. They were so many that they could hardly squeeze themselves into the room—but what are material walls to immaterial beings?

All bent over me to comfort me. I sensed how they caressed me with gentle love, and blessed me. Carefully I stood up and blessed them in return. I sang 'Om Bhur Bhuva Svaha...' as they stood in a circle around me and I dedicated to them the ones who were coming.

When, finally, I closed the door behind me for the last time, the rain had stopped and there was a soft sunset light in the garden, watery and mysterious.

Slowly I went round and everywhere I sang the Mantra. In some places I felt as if held back—then I stayed and sang it once more, comforting them that even though I was leaving, our Creator is not going anywhere.

Everywhere I thanked them, the beings I could sense but not see, and all the plant life, and I shared with them grief and nostalgia, but above all, gratitude.

My farewell.

Paradise Recreated

In shock I gazed around me. My heart sank as I squinted against the harsh light that reflected mercilessly on the whitewashed garden walls and the bare sand.

This time God had given us a barren place without a single plant or shrub, let alone a decent tree. Gone from our life were the magnificent old trees and the abundance of flowers. What was to be our garden was dry, hot sand with stones.

I had come to our new home in Botswana. The company, which had contracted Pieter, had rented a sweet little house for us in a newly developed area in the outskirts of the capital, Gabarone, and we were its first residents. Amazing by the way, how 'developing' usually means obliterating what has always existed. Beautiful landscapes, the original habitats for animals, a diversity of plant life, and sometimes humans have to give way for few to live where many were before.

Botswana, a country just north of South Africa, with Namibia west and Zimbabwe east of its borders, consists mainly of savannah and desert. The world-famous Okavango Delta is in the far northwestern part of the country.

The landscape around the capital is flat, with sudden hills rising up that are covered with vegetation of sparse low acacia trees, thorny shrubs, and dry, hard grasses, interspersed with stones.

Our house was at the foot of the Kgale Hill, which overlooks the southern part of Gabarone. The overall impression of the hill is dull, dry red-brown with green struggling to make its point, but a crown of huge boulders gives it an intriguing profile against the dark blue sky. Birds and butterflies make the air come alive with sound and movement and sweet wafts of wild thyme and basil scent the afternoon breeze. The whole has a rough primal, even mystical charm of its own that, in time, found its way into our hearts.

The Kgale Hill area was home to an extended baboon family, and now and then a huge silvery male came to sit on our garden wall for a while, mystified by what was happening to his territory. Luckily he never ventured any closer, for he made us feel uncomfortable and we stayed inside the house until he had left. Wild animals become aggressive and dangerous once they have found out that 'people' equals 'food lying around', as we had experienced in our early days in Kenya.

Exploring our new habitat on a Sunday morning, twenty years earlier, we had taken a walk along the river in the Nairobi game park in the small area where this was permitted. When we came back to the car, Costyn declared that he was hungry. Minding the signs, 'Do not feed the monkeys', we duly put him in the backseat of the car and closed the door before we gave him a banana. We never thought of closing the windows as well, and while we were getting in the car ourselves, like a flash of lightning, a young vervet monkey dashed in through the backseat window. It was a cute little animal with its black mask and white side-whiskers, but not on our three-year-old son's lap, fighting to get his banana. The monkey pulled, the child held on, and both screamed at the top of their voices. Very frightened, Costyn let go first and the monkey tore off to the closest available tree to enjoy its ill-gotten gains. It took us quite a while to calm down our child—and ourselves, for that matter.

At a safe distance, however, monkeys are wonderful. Daily the baboon clan appeared over the top of our Kgale hill. With the patriarch keeping watch at the very top, the others inspected the edibles like roots, berries, seeds, termites and lizards. When they were satisfied, the older ones sat down to rest and quietly contemplate life. The youngsters on the other hand, exploded in a circus-on-the-rocks. In sheer joy they jumped over the boulders, tumbled over the cliffs and swung in the trees on the lower part of the hill. Pulling any tail that came within their grasp, they chased each other around until the ensuing wrestling matches inevitably ended in a screeching fight. Then one of the elders would swing into action, and with snarls and swats the children were corrected into behaving until monkey order had returned.

Change is never far away.

A hot, lazy Sunday was coming to an end. The usual spectacular sunset was coloring the skies purple, orange, pink, blue, and gold, when the bush caught fire further down towards town. Gradually the smoke came creeping up our hill, obscuring the glowing colors in the sky. When the fire itself followed, the whole neighborhood sprung into nervous action. Shouting back and forth, everyone connected water hoses to their pool pumps and armed themselves with buckets and fire extinguishers. The owners of the homes at the edge were in the first line of danger and had already called the fire brigade.

In Nairobi, whenever we heard the sirens of the fire brigade, we used to say to each other, "Great, they are on their way to yesterday's fire." That was because they never had enough gasoline, or money for spare parts for the car, or they did not know the way, or they first had to go and find a hydrant to fill their tank. But luckily in Gabarone they were well organized and arrived in time to extinguish the fire on the side of the homes and keep everyone safe.

The next day the baboons appeared. They were obviously shaken by the violence of the fire, which had ravaged their habitat. Far and wide their food stores had been burned and their world as they had known it had died overnight. They seemed to be baffled by the sudden blackness of the earth, and listlessly they scampered over the stones. When finally the whole clan sat down, the patriarch on the top expressed what they all must have been feeling. His elbow resting on one knee and his hand under his chin, he sat staring over their habitat in mourning, sad as a tired old man.

Time and again events in the outer world seem to mirror back to us our life as an individual. The screams and the fighting of the baboons on the Kgale Hill could be interpreted as a manifestation of my own monkey mind. Holding on to the past and forgetting that there is an underlying order to all that presents itself as our lives, it kept jumping from fear to anger to grief to guilt and pain.

Of course we had not caused the fire, as little as we had provoked the financial disaster in which we lost everything. The fire had not reached us and we had not been in any real danger, but the state of the hill with its animals reflected the essence of our lives at that moment—bare and lost.

Economic necessity had forced us to leave Kenya, the country that had been home for so long. In the order of things, our son had left for Europe to pursue further education, and we missed him. We had had to let go of our magic home on the top of the hill and all the people we loved.

We had lost our habitat, as we had known it. Uprooted, economically and emotionally shattered, we had to find our food elsewhere. Sharing the territory of another clan, we had to search for the seeds and berries of new work, friendships and inspiration. We had to learn to relate to the new land and its peoples. We were in mourning as the landscape itself.

Little by little, however, as the trees and the shrubs began to unfold new leaves and the resilient hard, dry grasses sprouted beneath the ashes, our spirit revived in us. We furnished the house, which was lovely. It had a sitting room in the shape of an extended bay-widow, as if to soften the transition from living in a round house into a square one.

We took a new puppy. We befriended our hospitable Botswana neighbors and they told us about their land and their culture. I learnt Ikebana, the artistic Japanese flower arranging that is so similar to painting in creating beautiful lines with just a few branches and two or three flowers—very challenging in a country where flowers hardly grow.

I was blessed to find friends, soul mates in art and spirituality. Soon, happy and slightly perplexed, I found myself teaching 'A Course in Miracles' in the savannah. On a chicken farm in the hills outside Gabarone, I learned the energies of the human Light Body, our spiritual energy-body that far exceeds the physical one. Pieter had a harder task, finding his way into the workings of the minds of the Motswana, as different from the Kenyans as the Eskimos from the Greek.

The Kgale hill was sacred to the Motswana. In the evening, as the Milky Way began to sparkle over the earth, often the voice of a man joined the sounds of the African darkness and chanted monotonous prayers deep into the night.

This mystical voice of the ancient soul of Africa made me feel an outsider, in a way, but at the same time awoke in me an awareness of unity. Many times I joined in with my own prayers, and then the singer and I met in adoring the Creator whom we all share as the Ground of our being. Then I connected the singing priest with my Christ Consciousness, and allowed him to deepen my love for the God of the African soul and soil—so intimately amalgamated.

The builders had left one single, smallish tree standing to provide shade for the terrace when they constructed the house, but apart from some tough weeds, the garden was bare. During the day, the unrelenting sun heated the dry, red-brown soil and stones to become like an oven surrounding the house.

The owner invited a landscape architect to design a garden and a few weeks later the man came up with a lovely design. The landlord approved, and the architect announced that he was now going go order the plants he needed and would start the work in three weeks time. Then, one week before he was to begin the work, we received a letter saying he was so sorry, but he had landed a more profitable job and he kindly advised us to approach one of the other landscape firms in town.

So, the procedure had to start from scratch again, and this meant a delay we could not afford. The one half of the year that produces a rain shower once in a while, was about to come to an end, and during the next six months the sky would not release a single drop of water to support new plant life. If we did not want to look at this desert for a long, long time to come, something urgently needed to be done.

The landlord knew that we loved gardening and, after a few days of deliberation, together we decided to do the job without professional help. We slightly redesigned the plans, more suitable to our wishes and the landlord's purse, and he organized ten workers with a foreman. He left choosing and buying the plants as well as supervising the planting to us. We were excited about the challenge, and within a week we got off to a flying start.

Soon, trucks with good soil drove in and out and, with thundering noise, unloaded stones for the rock garden. All over, people were digging, planting and watering, and the garden was filled with activity and noise. For thousands of years the Motswana have been shouting to each other across long distances in desert and savannah, and the power of the workmen's voices was impressive. The birds kept a respectful distance from this pandemonium.

The neighbor had a tree, a proper one, and half of its branches reached into our garden. One day halfway through the work, Pieter and I stood looking at what was coming into being, dreaming of the garden's glorious future. It was lunchtime, the workers had gone off to eat, and in the sudden, eerie silence, a little nondescript bird alighted high on a tree branch that was hanging over our wall. Facing us, it began to sing. It burst out in a cascade of jubilant rollers and trills, and, as it showered us in sound, it seemed to bless the garden and us with its song.

A gentle breeze caressed our faces. God speaks in the prayers on the mountain at night and in the play of the baboons, in the whispering of the wind and in the song of the birds. For a second, paradise opened and I knew that this little creature celebrated our presence and our work. Its exuberance sang,

"Thank you for what you are doing.

"Thank you, we are so happy!"

The man, who so disgracefully had let us down, had listened to the nudging of Mother Earth. She did not want him to make her garden, but us, with our love and our understanding of nature and her invisible helpers.

O yes, they are there—the elves, the gnomes and the nymphs—these little brothers and sisters of the angels who are more than a product of human imagination. Through the ages, people have seen them clairvoyantly, the salamanders, the sylphs and the undines—spirits of fire, air and water that live in fairytales and folktales.

Although they do not have dense material bodies and our senses usually are not refined enough to perceive them, even today some of us can sense or see them in their energy bodies. I had discovered them through my painting. For many years I have used a technique, which allows room to play for more than myself alone.

First, I apply splashes of watercolor or acrylic paint on a glass plate. Then, while the paint is still wet, I put a sheet of paper on the glass and rub it gently all over with both hands. When I feel the paper has soaked up enough paint, I pull it off and quickly lay it flat on the floor, careful not to make the wet paint run.

This is a creative process of great freedom. Instead of starting off with defining forms, the first initiative is mine in that I provide the colors on the glass. But then I hand it over to the water and the paper and the paint—only to take the process in hand again when the paper and the paint are dry.

And this is where the real creative challenge begins. The water has made the colors mix and flow into beautiful shades and shapes. As I turn the paper over to study the result from all sides, I discover vague shapes—of hidden mountains, lakes and trees, of kings, fairies and angels, dolphins, birds and butterflies.

With watercolor pencil I work back into it, to bring out the forms that water and paint have given me, to create depth, and to bring harmony in the color structure. This part of the process can take days or weeks or months—even years—and often, as the painting grows, I discover more hidden worlds and beings.

Surrounded by the radiant light of Nairobi and the abundant plant and animal life in and around the house, painting for me had become a process of co-creating. Water is a familiar and accessible element to spiritual beings, so while the paper is on the glass and soaks up the colors, 'anyone' can slip in and have his or her moment of creation.

In Nairobi, they were enthusiastic participants and they loved to make their presence known. They portrayed themselves in naughty eyes looking over the edge of a cloud or from behind a tuft of grass. I found a gnome asleep in a hollow under the surface of the earth, tired of his work of being the middleman between the minerals of the soil and the roots of the plants. A huge fire spirit danced in a bushfire, undines floated above water and fairies hovered over flowers, a winged horse, birds.... Even magnificent night blue and purple angels have appeared, and everywhere vague human figures adored the light I nearly always keep as the center of a painting.

Angels and nature beings, or elementals, are different expressions of divine consciousness. We humans live and grow through experiencing resistance and opposites, but they live and grow in the flow of divine harmony—all part of an immense hierarchy in which each and everyone has a task to perform. They are the helpers of the planetary intelligence inside the body of the earth. And they are all around us.

The water nymphs live in the watery element of the air. In a dreamlike state of consciousness, they bind and unbind the elements of the air and enter them into the leaves. Their home is where water and air touch. Did you ever wonder why a water drop sparkles so much at the tip of a blade of grass? It is a nymph in bliss, playing on its surface.

Did you ever sit in nature and, half closing your eyes, wonder about these pinpoints of light that run towards you like excited snowflakes? Might they be the sylphs on their way to carry the light into the plants?

The fire spirits—their ancient name is salamander, because in the past people thought these little creatures were born from the fire—gather the warmth in the air and carry its workings into the plants.

The gnomes—the players in so many stories we tell our children—are the conductors of the orchestra. They are the ones who receive the offerings of the nymphs, the sylphs and the fire spirits. Caretakers of the plants inside the earth, they inspire them to grow in summer, and in winter, they help to prepare them for a new life.

Oh, the beauty which is there to see when we take our mind out of our head and our body out of the car. When we sit in nature and dream and look with the eyes of our heart, then it is no longer difficult to imagine the butterflies to be the thoughts of the plants, or to see how the flowers dream of flying off in the warm air. The butterflies are longing to enter the warm moist soil, the womb of all plant life, the body of Mother Earth, and whenever they touch a flower, they experience their desires fulfilled. They feel complete. They have found heaven on earth.

Won't we clap our hands in delight when we see the fire spirits riding the tiny spaceships of the pollen?

The birds never fly alone. They are the great love of the sylphs. And in the music of the air stream that follows their flight—which we can imagine we hear—the sylphs are in bliss.

In the area of our new home, nature's beings had never worked together with humans. On the contrary, these two-legged giants ruthlessly chased them away with bulldozers and pesticides, and changed everything they had ever known. Their confusion must have been great.

Man's wishes would be difficult to understand for the beings that were going to care for the gardens in this new neighborhood. The 'overseers'—devas—of animal species like worms and insects also needed to learn to communicate with humans. We were honored with the task to give form to the small area within our garden wall and to show the invisible world how to cooperate in creating a new situation for all—a beautiful garden. The invitation to be their guide and teacher, conveyed by the little bird in the neighbor's tree, filled me with excitement and joy.

The garden began to take shape. The laborers worked hard and fast, but they were unfamiliar with planting trees in the poor Botswana soil. They had to dig man-deep holes, fill them up with good soil mixed with compost and plenty of water, and put in the tree not too deep, nor too high. I had to constantly monitor them.

They planted climbers and creepers along the white garden wall to soften the stark light that hurt the eyes, and they dug flowerbeds. They made a rock garden. This actually was the least ambitious of our plans! Succulents and cacti are indigenous and in harmony with soil and climate—which was not exactly the case with the stem-roses we planted at the side of the swimming pool.

When all this was done, they brought in rolls of mature grass to cover the well prepared and soaking wet soil.

The ants were delighted. This was room service at its best. They called in the whole tribe and collectively they feasted on the nice juicy roots. And morning after morning we woke up, appalled to see big areas that had become brown overnight.

I talked to them. They did not hear. I gently talked to their deva. I explained that I respected the fact that this area had been theirs forever, but that we were going to share it from now on. We wanted nice, cool grass and would they kindly move to the plot next door that was still wild? They are a dense little lot, so unfortunately they did not get it. In the end I had to make a clear statement and, recommending them to love, we sprayed the grass.

I had more luck with some fantastical, prehistoric beetles, which were eating the buds of the hibiscus flowers. Many mornings, I took them off by hand, one by one, and sent them flying over the wall to the empty plot next door. Sometimes I boiled chili peppers in water and sprayed the plants with the tea to repel them, all the while explaining that these flowers were the first messengers of the colors I was yearning for in my new garden. In the end they seemed to understand that they were not welcome and they stayed away.

My special pet was an enormous millipede. He always appeared when I watered the garden, eager to catch a drop. It was fascinating to watch his five-inch long, shiny black body artfully move on those countless little legs. He lived in the garden, but one afternoon I came back from shopping and, to my surprise, met him on the road. Slowly, he came crossing over from the opposite neighbors over the hot tarmac:

"Oh, there you are," I called as I opened my car window. "You are coming home, are you? You'd better watch the traffic, it's getting close to rush hour!"

The one tree we had was a marula, a tree that yields dark yellow fruits, the size of a small plum. They had gotten ripe before we started our ambitious gardening project, and when they began to drop off, I did not throw them away. I swept them together in a heap on the terrace, instead, in order to have some color. Their soft skin lit up in a delicate orange glow.

These juicy fruits ferment when they get overripe and gradually the air filled with a prickly aroma of alcohol. In South Africa, they are used to make a sweet liqueur, aptly named Amarula, but they are a delicacy for the animals, too.

During our first marula season, we were having our supper on the terrace, one night, when Mr. Millipede came crawling over the fruit heap for his evening season snack—or drink.

Fascinated, we watched how he gripped the silky fruits with his thousand feet and heaved himself slowly up to the top of the mound. He sniffed around to decide on the most delectable marula, and then set off again over the hills and vales until he could sink his tiny teeth in the elected fruit.

He had his fill and we were having ours. Pieter told me about his day in the ministry and I amused him with latest heroics and histrionics of the puppy. We looked down to see how Mr. Millipede was doing at the marula heap.

"He is still eating," Pieter remarked. But as we looked closer, I said,

"Look, that's funny! He is not moving at all."

"Can you believe it?" Pieter exclaimed. "He is asleep, right there, on top of the fruits."

Mr. Millipede was relaxed, however, as no animal would ever be in the open air, unprotected from predators. With all his thousand little legs motionless, he was hanging head down over the fruits. And slowly it dawned on our amazed minds that he was completely drunk!

Botswana is one of the world's foremost producers of gem quality diamonds. I never saw one, but the effect of this wealth is visible in the care the government takes of even the poorest, the investment made in educating the youth, and the widespread information on Aids. This in itself was a new experience for us.

I could never afford any diamonds, of course, but I am infinitely more intrigued and fascinated by crystals, anyway.

We had brought our collection with us. Our most striking piece is a priceless smoky quartz crystal. A proud obelisk, it stands fifteen inches tall, and it is more unique than diamonds. It is smoky brown in color and at the same time perfectly clear. The sides, as well as the facets at the top that form the apex, are covered with mysterious figures and signs that seem to convey ancient wisdom contained in the crystal. I always feel as if I can 'read' them but the meaning forever slips away just beyond my understanding.

Beach sand sparkles bright in the sunlight with formless specks of quartz. Under the right geological circumstances, however, minerals develop perfect geometrical forms. The quartz family for instance, with clear quartz, smoky, rose quartz and purple amethyst, forms elongated six sided crystals with an apex of six facets, in rare instances even up to ten.

The sides of the thin black or deep green tourmaline wands are finely striated, with perfect little triangles at the apex. The fascinating fluorite family comes in triangles or double pyramids in transparent green, white, mauve, purple or golden. Deep red garnet manifests in a small twelve-sided crystal with diamond-shaped facets, and the metal pyrite in heavy, solid, gold-colored rectangular cubes.

In their diversity of form, color, and chemical substance they are like different personalities. They are a challenge to the scientific mind and a feast for the eye, but to the heart they all mirror back a single message,

"We are as God created us. Neither time nor external circumstances have touched us since our formation. We are as pure in expression as we were in the beginning of our creation."

Our Smoky has come to us unbroken and undamaged over the millions of years of its formation, and it is always treated with reverence and care. Its dark color conveys that it belongs to the earth, but at the same time the light of its perfect clarity is heaven. The crystal is a statement from the mineral kingdom that light and dark, earth and heaven can exist within one single material expression, in balance, beauty, defenselessness and power.

I meditated daily in a quiet corner of the house, away from the distractions of housework, telephone, TV or computer.

I played and experimented with Smoky. I put it on a small table in front of me and sat staring at it, its beauty a source of marvel and joy. I closed both hands around it to feel its cool touch and let my fingers probe the symbols on the surface, inviting them to yield their secrets. I put it on the floor, right under the spine, my own physical central connection between earth and heaven, to remind it to heal.

One morning, I withdrew with my ancient friend into my meditation corner to take refuge from the sunlight, which, even inside the house, was blinding on the whitewashed garden wall. I held it in my hands and I let my active mind sink deep into the eternal silence of the stone.

As earth and heaven are one in the dark-clear crystal, so they are in us and we in them. As usual, I put Smoky on the floor, under my chair, to invite a clear connection between earth, heaven and myself. I closed my eyes. And in this stillness I began to see:

I sink deep into the earth. If it would physically open up and my body was about to disappear, I would be scared to death, but my immaterial consciousness and love cannot be threatened, so I surrender to the sense of love and protection that Mother Earth conveys.

As long as we walk her surface, even her deepest depths are rooms of our home. She is the womb without which no life can be born. Nurturing, protecting, loving and flowing, she makes new what is old and brings life to death. Sister to stars and galaxies, she births stones and soil and rain and sustains us all from her substance.

For a little while, I enjoy her loving embrace. Then, from within the body and the-day-to-day mind, in stillness and surrender I move into a different level of consciousness. Weightless I soar up, free of the aches and pains of the body that I leave behind in the chair.

Through the blues of our sky, I move towards luminous cobalt, this energetic blue in between light and dark, where I see an iridescent light beckon me in the far distance

As I approach it, I begin to distinguish shapes of crystal-like, translucent, square buildings. I am deeply moved when I recognize them. Those are the ones I often paint, without knowing why, but with a profound sense of belonging.

It is an actual city. It exists in form in a place in consciousness of a less dense energy, real, but not material as we know it. It is a place, which apparently I have always known, but cannot see with my physical eyes unless I bring it out in a painting.

I come home.

As I look around in wonder, light-beings come pouring in from all sides. And in the sudden atmosphere of celebration, I sense their delight at my visit.

They take me by the hand and, enchanted, I follow them in a walk through the town. The shape of the buildings is elongated tall, with flat roofs, and they stand alone or in clusters.

Here and there we are invited into a house that fills with light when we enter, and I feel like meeting neighbors and friends and relatives after a long stay away.

I fold my hands in grateful prayer and I look up. Then I see him, Jesus, shimmering above the crystal houses. A grand Being of light, he enfolds the town but, at the same time, it seems to come flowing out of him—a place created by him for his own. I fall at his feet.

I praise him, thank him and love him. I pray that he may expand my consciousness ever further to see and to understand, and then I merge with him.

As we seem to radiate outward, he takes me soaring up to the stars and through their constellations to the edges of this universe. Beyond it lies another one, all white, golden yellow and fiery red. We enter it and I am ecstatic. This is home to my fireside and I want to stay and live there. But he moves onward and higher again.

We move into a universe of night-dark, profound silence. The Place of Silent Being is where he has taken me. And here we stay.

All excitement leaves me. I become still and I pray,

"This is where I want to be. From here I want to work on earth. From this silence of I Am comes the Voice for God to us. It spoke to Moses in the burning bush, it spoke in the prophets and the gospel writers, and it speaks in us all when words of love leave our heart and mouth. Here is the wisdom that cannot be learned by senses and matter-bound mind. It lights up in us at times; and when it does, we know not where it comes from."

This holy Place is at great distance and at the same time deep within us. I vow to Jesus that I will train my mind and my emotions ever more to go into this silence of my being where God says, 'Be still and know that I Am God'— and let him speak.

This sacred moment passes. He takes me back to the crystal city in the cobalt blue sky.

The contrast is great but joyful. The streets are filled with activity and happy beings are busy decorating everything with orange garlands. The air seems to vibrate with laughter. It is the celebration of my homecoming.

I walk through the streets and I come to a hall of learning. I feel drawn to enter. A venerable old being comes forward to greet me and I bow down in reverence to touch his feet, but he makes me stand up and says,

"There is no need, you are one of us," and he embraces me in an embrace of ancient wisdom.

"Tomorrow we will talk," he promises me, "today is for celebration."

Back outside, my light family takes me by the hand once more, and—how well they know me—proud and happy they walk me to a pleasure garden of radiant white light.

Here are the ancient trees I have missed so much, singing in the wind with birds and rustling leaves. Luscious green lawns, sprinkled with flowerbeds, weave themselves around them. Some areas are left to the wild flowers— poppies, cornflowers, red campion and evening primrose. I do not see colors as we know them, but I sense them. The shapes in radiant light emanate qualities of color and vibrate in the splendor of this magnificent park.

My nature beings flash through my mind. Are they sending me a message? I take my awareness back to my earthly home and to the self, which sits in the chair in the corner of my meditation room. Without ever opening my eyes, I invite them,

"Come children, do come with me if you like."

From all sides they come streaming in, the fairies and the gnomes, the devas of the worms, the birds, the bees and the beetles, and the sylphs and nymphs. And when my heart tells me that we are complete, I take them by the hand and we soar up.

In the split second of a thought we are back in the crystal city, where the air soon tinkles with the laughter of delight of my brothers and sisters when they see them.

Enchanted nature's children are taken to the garden. And as they take in the sight unfolding before their eyes, they stand motionless in wonder.

Then, all at once, they explode in a bubble of excitement. Like lightning, they flash in all directions and they want to be everywhere at the same time. They throw handfuls of light high up in the air and splash it around like water, all the while laughing in exuberant joy.

I see little Jorra coming in the distance, my longhaired Jack Russell terrier who, for fourteen years, shared my life in Nairobi, never more than three steps away from me if she could help it. With her triangular ears flapping, she runs as fast as her little legs can move. She had died before we had to leave Kenya, and now, to my delight, she is here! And, just as she did on earth, she runs around in circles, ecstatic to have found me in this place. She jumps up and down and takes bites out of the light that seems to dance around her; she rolls over in it...

Finally, all are done frolicking and their excitement subsides. Jorra lies down, panting and alert with her bright eyes, and with tenderness we watch the nature beings as they sit down in a circle. They have forgotten us now, and they are completely absorbed in deliberating what to do with the experience. I see their thought energies and ideas flash back and forth, and when they seem to have reached a decision, they quietly stand up.

They look around as if to make their choice in the abundance. In wonder we see how, with delicate fingers, they each take a drop of light from their chosen tree, plant, or flower—some even from the soil itself—and place it reverently in their heart. All now shine with a drop of light in their hearts!

I then sense their urge to return to work. I take them back to earth and they tell me,

"You give us the water and we will do the rest!" and then they disappear in flash. They now know what to do.

Is it amazing that, in less than a year, our papaya tree had sixty fruits clutching to its young, slender stem, or that the basil plants grew into shrubs, or that one clear morning, I found woven in its branches a spider web of pure gold?

And Then One Day

After we had lived in Botswana for a little over six months, I wrote this letter to our extended soul-family all over the world:

Dear Friends,

Last Thursday we came back from Johannesburg, where Pieter was in the hospital for eight days. His life has been saved by brilliant medical science, but above all by the grace of God!

I wish to share with you what has happened to us recently.

Saturday two weeks ago, at six in the morning, Pieter woke me up. He said:

"I am not feeling well." My stomach tightened. He is always well and he never wakes me up.

"I think I want to go to the hospital," he said with an apprehensive tone in his voice.

"All right," I tried to wake up my mind as well as my body, "I'll get dressed and get the car out."

"You'd better call an ambulance," he answered, "I think it is my heart."

Now panic gripped me and I shot out of bed.

We have lived in Botswana for only six months, and you know how it takes time to discover how everything is organized in a new country. Moreover, there had never been any sign that we should be prepared for this kind of emergency.

"I have no idea how to get one! What number do we have to call?"

"Call the security company. They will tell you," he had the presence of mind to say.

Luckily the number was on the cover of the panic button in the sitting room, so that was easy, which was just as well as I was very nervous by then. With trembling fingers, I dialed. A kind man answered the phone and gave me the number of an ambulance service that would respond swiftly.

I got through to them all right, but it appeared too complicated to explain how they could find our street. They were not familiar with the newly constructed area where we live, and the fastest way to get them to the house would be for me to go out and meet them at the petrol station at the nearest shopping center.

I was very distressed to leave Pieter in the middle of what later appeared to be a heart attack, but I got into the car and left. When I reached my destination a few minutes later, no one was there yet. Distraught I paced up and down for what seemed to be hours, and then a medical officer arrived in a saloon car.

Again I panicked. "Where is the ambulance?" I asked the man.

"It is on its way, but it has to come from much farther away than I. Don't worry, I have all the necessary emergency equipment with me here in the car," he added reassuringly.

We came back to the house, where Pieter was sitting in the lounge in his pajamas, with a very nervous puppy at his feet. The medical officer got his instruments out and began to assess the situation.

In the meantime, the driver of the ambulance called and he, too, asked for directions. He did not know the way either. And once more the fastest way to get him to the house was to meet him at a place he knew. Hurriedly I left home for a second time. This time I felt less awful that I had to leave Pieter. At least someone was taking care of him now, and I only had to drive a few streets this time.

From then on, it all went very fast. Within ten minutes they had done their checkup and laid Pieter on a stretcher. They carried him in the ambulance and told me the name of the hospital where they were going to take him.

"I don't know this hospital," I said. "I'm new here and I don't know anything in this town. I'll have to follow you."

Anxiously I added, "Please, do make sure not to lose me in the traffic?"

The morning was cloudy and gray, as befitted the occasion. When we arrived at the hospital, only the crows, coarsely crowing in the trees, gave a sign of being happy with the new day.

By then it was seven o'clock, so where I had not even known where to begin, I had managed to get him into a hospital within an hour's time.

He was put on a bed in Casualty. A nurse drew the curtain around us, and a very tired lady doctor, at the end of her night shift, came to examine him and make another electrocardiogram.

She did not say much, but by the time she left with her readings we were not too worried anymore. The pain was gone and Pieter was feeling a lot better. Above all, he was safely in the hospital. We had the feeling that we had made it in time and that nothing serious could go wrong. Little did we know....

After a while, I got restless and I went in search of the doctor. I found her and she told me that she had discussed the ECG with a colleague.

"It was a heart attack all right," she informed me. "I'm afraid we will have to keep him in Intensive Care for a while to see how he develops."

Shocked, I went back to Pieter and told him the news.

"Mmm," he said, "I had just decided that it was only a stomach upset, after all," as this was the area where he had experienced the initial pain. "It is really my heart then?"

It was not easy to take in the fact that something was seriously wrong with this man, who was always so strong and healthy. We waited for further proceedings and talked quietly.

Over the years, he had witnessed my evolving into a spiritual healer and together we had changed and expanded our view on life, death, and life after death as a soul. It was a reality for us that our souls make the choice to come to earth and, on a super-conscious level, also decide, together with God, when the time has come to move on.

Softly I asked him:

"Do you feel you have finished your mission on earth? Do you want to go or do you want to stay on?"

"I'd like to stay. There is so much to enjoy in life and I feel that I still have a task," he answered,

I put my left hand on his heart and my right one on his stomach, and softly I began to pray the Gayatri mantra:

"Om Bhur Buvahasvaha. Oh God, Source of all Light and all Life...."

I tuned in to the powerful energy of these ancient sacred words, which, over thousands of years, have been prayed by lay people and priests alike. I had sung them countless times, and I had grown to be one with the holy sounds. Now I was praying them aloud with Pieter, and for him.

All of a sudden he shot upright. He clutched his stomach and cried out,

"Call a nurse; I am in such pain!" and then he fell backward on the bed.

"Nurse!" I screamed. She was in the cubicle next to ours. She turned around, yanked the curtain aside to see what was happening, and immediately pressed an alarm bell that made nurses and doctors come running. In one move they rushed in, pushed me out, and closed the curtain again.

And there I stood—forlorn, terrified, and in shock, in the middle of a public place where other patients were being brought in. I knew he was dying and they had made me leave him. Only a simple curtain divided me from my dying husband and I was not allowed to be with him.

A young girl, probably a nurse in training, came in.

I grabbed both her arms. "Are you a nurse?" I cried, trembling. "He is dying. Oh my God, I don't want to lose him! I love him so much. God, help us!"

Gently she pushed me to a door.

"Come with me," she said.

"NO! I must stay here, I have to be close to him."

She then took me to a simple wooden bench in the corridor close by, and quietly sat down next to me. Doctors and nurses were running back and forth, but I could do nothing but wait. I felt sick and dazed by the sudden turn of events. It all had gone so fast.

My natural reaction to disaster is to pray, but in shock the mind does not work and so I repeated incessantly only three words, the name of the Lord,

"Jay Sai Ram— Hail my Father-Mother God—Jay Sai Ram, Jay Sai Ram".

After what seemed an eternity, someone came to inform me that that the heart was 'fluttering', but that Pieter was still alive and that they were now going to move him to Intensive Care.

The young nurse took me upstairs. She left as I sat down on a bench outside the door of Intensive Care, but immediately another nurse joined me.

"I will stay with you," she said as she sat down.

"Don't you have your work to do?" I asked, knowing how hectic a hospital is in the early morning.

"I delegated my work to someone else," divine Love answered calmly. I have never known the name of this sweet person and I never saw her again after that morning.

I was cold with fear.

"Let us pray together," she urged. Craving for physical human warmth, I took her hands and together we prayed to our beloved Jesus. I do not remember what I said to him; only the soothing murmur of her voice, talking to the Lord, comes back to my memory.

Every once in a while, nurses came out of the door and always assured us that the heart was beating, although 'fluttering'. During the whole of this eternity of waiting, while I was ceaselessly praying, the nurse stayed with me. She held my hand and she comforted me that Jesus was with us—as my heart knew to be true.

After she left me for a short while, I became unbearably nervous. I got up and frantically I began to pace up and down the gray corridor. Suddenly I felt very strange. Shivering, nauseous and dizzy, I seemed about to faint, but it did not come from inside my body.

It was not I. Somehow I sensed that I was experiencing the pull of Pieter's being, and I knew that he was holding on to me—to stay, or to say farewell?

At that moment the nurse returned. Trembling and with the tears streaming over my face, I sobbed,

"He is dying; he is going now. I feel it."

"Let us pray again," she urged.

"I can't," I wept, "you pray, I can't."

She held my hands tightly in hers and prayed with great intensity,

"Dear Lord Jesus, be with him. His life is in your hands; it is yours. Please give us strength. We know that you never leave us, and that you are always blessing us in the Father. Let your love prevail. Heavenly Father God, we ask you to be with Pieter, in the name of our Lord Jesus."

A few minutes later I was called in. The doctor came to meet me. He was small in stature, very black, and he had large, brown, compassionate eyes. He told me that Pieter had had four heart attacks, with each time a cardiac arrest; the first one of which had happened in Casualty while I was with him. Each time, when the effect of the stabilizing medication had been exhausted, the heart had stopped and four times they had had to reanimate him.

"There is nothing more we can do now," he said with grief in his eyes. "The next time will be the last."

A strange numbness came over me. I needed to hold on to someone, so I took his hands.

"I know, just now in the corridor I sensed that he was going," I said, ice-cold with dismay.

"But don't lose hope," divine love in his heart made him say, "God can do miracles." He looked into my eyes and I could see this came from deep within him.

I went to the bed and looked at Pieter. His breathing was irregular and difficult; he was struggling for his life.

I hugged him. I stammered a few words of farewell, and then I laid my hands on him and prayed,

"Our Father who is in heaven,
Hallowed be your Name,
Your kingdom come,
Your will be done,
On earth as in heaven...

All joined me in my prayer, the doctor, the nurses, and God knows, maybe even the hearts of the premature-born babies who were lying in their incubator in the same room; love is omnipresent and does not depend on the mind being fully present on earth. And together we waited for the next and final heart attack. We waited for him to die.

Long minutes followed.

I was aware that we can prevent our loved ones from leaving the body, even if this is what they desire. By physically holding a dying person, in grief, and in the fear that we cannot live without him, we can actually prevent the soul from leaving the body. And it is great, selfless love to go beyond our own pain and anxiety and give the dying person the permission to go.

I did not hold him; I did not keep my hands on him; I concentrated on setting him free. I softly talked to him. Even though he was unconscious, I knew his soul would hear me.

"I want you to follow the mission of your soul. Go with God and make your choice of the highest love. I will support you, even if it means that Costyn and I will have to live on without you."

This was not easy. I had to wrench this surrender from the depth of my being.

"We will miss you so much, but we will manage somehow. Thank you for your love and your presence in our lives. Thank you for all you have given us. Love is eternal and limitless, and you are a part of us as we are part of you. We will never really be separated."

The first hour, I paced around the bed with my hands folded in prayer, 'Jai Sai Ram, Jai Sai Ram,' or I sat at his side, close, but without touching him. Praying for his soul, I could only hold on to God.

The doctor was very worried about possible brain damage that might have been caused by the lack of oxygen during the repeated cardiac arrests. Passionately I assured him that I did not want Pieter to live as an invalid, physically or mentally.

"He is such a free spirit and he has worked so hard for the good of mankind; he does not deserve it," I said with fervor. "I don't want that for him. Let him go!"

The doctor nodded understandingly, but after some time he started to connect a drip. Fiercely, I asked,

"What are you doing now?"

"I have to try, at least for twenty-four hours," he replied.

I knew I had to accept this. Of course, it was his duty and his responsibility as a physician to continue trying.

Another hour of anxiety passed. I asked the doctor if I could call my friend in Nairobi from the ICU, as I did not want to go downstairs and leave Pieter. He agreed and arranged for me to be allowed to call abroad.

Thank God Janet was in and, in tears, I told her what was happening.

"Janet, he is dying," I sobbed.

"Who? Who is dying?"

"Pieter. I am in ICU here, in Gabarone. I need you. I need Baba. I need everyone in Nairobi to pray for us!"

After she got over the initial shock, she told me she began to see Sai Baba standing at the head of Pieter's bed.

"I will help," she heard him promise us.

This strengthened me. I knew that he would help Pieter either to die, notwithstanding the medical support, or get better. He did not tell me which way it would go, as this was the choice Pieter's soul was in the process of making. It also was my challenge of faith; it was the test of my love for my husband and my willingness to surrender him to God.

Janet promised to call the Sai group in Nairobi, as well as many of our other friends. It comforted me to know that it would not be long before many people would be praying for Pieter, for us. Even though they were far away, it made me feel less alone in this place.

Around eleven I tried to call Costyn in Holland.

"I have to ask him to come over," I told the doctor. "If I call now, at least I will be honest when I tell him his father is ill, but alive."

It took me more then twenty minutes to get through to him. God's love works in every detail. It had made sure that Costyn was not alone and some friends had just arrived at his place when my call came. Even though I had to tell him that his father was very ill, I was very careful not to let him know what was really going on, as he would have to travel twenty long hours to reach us.

Unconscious, but alive, Pieter continued to struggle. I sat with him for some more hours, praying and softly talking to him in case he could hear me. My thoughts went out to all those I knew who had lost their spouses in exactly the same way, and I knew it was a very real possibility that this was happening to me now.

The medical staff had some treatment to do and I decided to go home for a while. I needed to inform the family. I had to eat something, and we had left the house so unprepared that I had not been able to arrange care for the puppy. I had left it locked up in the house and it needed food and a walk in the garden.

My way home led past Pieter's office in the Ministry. A colleague had just arrived from Europe and I went in and ran upstairs, praying that he would be in. I needed support so badly.

He was there and, my words choking my throat, I told him what was happening. He, too, was deeply shaken. He is not in the least religious, but later he told me that he had prayed after I had left again. Pieter got even the non-believers to pray!

No one can imagine how it is to have something so grave happen in a country where you hardly know anyone. This was a shock on top of a shock.

Once I was home, I called our doctor-friend in Nairobi who had lost his beloved wife in the same way. When he got over the shock of his emotions, he assured me that Pieter would be all right because they had worked on him from the very first moment. The blood flow to the brain would never have stopped altogether long enough to have the dreaded effect of brain damage.

"He will be all right," he said as much from his heart as from his medical experience.

I took courage from his words, because I knew from experience the truth of his medical knowledge as well as his intuition. A deeply devoted Muslim, I knew he would support us with his prayers to Allah.

Just ten days before it all happened, God had given me a friend here in Botswana. An artist and a healer like me, she has God and the Christ in the center of her being in the same way as I do. She lives outside of town on a farm similar to the one I had left behind in Nairobi. From the very first moment we had felt at home together, as if we had known each other forever—which probably is the truth.

I called her and asked her to pray for us, and she offered Reiki healing as well as any practical help she could give. This made me feel better; at least there was someone for me now close by.

After I had talked to our priest friend in America, I sensed strength flowing to me from the power of his prayers. And, in my profound need to share what I was going through, I quickly sent out a short email to friends elsewhere in the world. How infinitely blessed we are. In a short period of time, Christians, Muslims, Hindus and unbelievers were praying for us in Europe, India, the United States and above all, Africa.

The remainder of the day I sat with Pieter. He was still alive and the doctor spoke with respect of his strength to fight on for his life. I now held him. I prayed. I talked to him. Above all, I continuously released him and surrendered him to the Father.

"Father, he is in your hands; He is yours. Your will be done. I surrender him to you, I only want his soul to live the highest love, be it on earth or in heaven."

In the next hours, I always had my hands on him. They were warm and tingling with the love of Jesus that was flowing into him as healing energy. Even in the days that followed, the heat never ceased to stream out of my hands; they were always 'working'. And whenever I left him, on my way out I dedicated this healing energy to the entire hospital,

The time went by so slowly, but with each passing hour the doctor had a little more hope that Pieter would survive. Tired and in despair, I rested my head on the bed and cried. The doctor passed by and he put a gentle hand on my shoulder. He said,

"Do not cry, you have been so strong all this time." It felt as if the hand of Jesus himself was comforting me.

Around four o'clock in the afternoon, I was exhausted but alert at the same time, when I heard a voice in my head ask clearly,

"Do you want him back?"

"Only if he can be happy," was my immediate response.

And this now was my pact with God. If he would live, I knew that he would not come back to be an invalid on this earth.

Towards evening, the doctor offered me a room in the hospital for the night. They might still have to call me back, and then I would have to drive the long distance in the dark all alone.

I woke up very early in the morning after a restless sleep, and I realized that no one had come to call me and that he was still with us. My hope increased. I went to intensive care, where he was still unconscious, and I talked to him for a while. Then I went home to shower, change and have some breakfast. I called the family to inform them of the situation and fed and reassured Tosha, the bewildered puppy.

The sun was rising when I drove back to the hospital again. A glorious huge orange ball illuminated the whole of the sky. For me, dressed in the color of Sai Baba's robe, it was a messenger from God. It spoke to me of more than hope; it promised me new life.

In the course of the morning, Pieter regained consciousness, and how profoundly moved and happy we all were. Even his reflexes seemed all right. As it was my contract with God that he should be whole and healthy if he came back to life, from that moment on, I never worried that he would be impaired in any way or that he would still get another attack and die. I believe Jesus when he said that the Father does not give his children a stone when they ask for bread, and I had complete trust now in

Pieter's full recovery. Love is perfect and God does not do half work.

When Costyn arrived at three in the afternoon, I could tell him that his father was out of danger.

The long and the short is that a miracle happened, according to the doctors and the nurses. On Monday morning, doctors who had heard about Pieter, came to see him and the nurses from Casualty,, who had been present on Saturday morning, rushed in when they came back to work.

"We have to see you and talk to you; we can't believe this. We were so sure you could not survive."

Pieter does not recall anything; he had been unconscious for over twenty-four hours, and on Sunday afternoon the doctor had to tell him what had happened. He assured Pieter that my faith and my prayers had saved him. Over and over again, he said the same thing to me, but I always added, "...and the prayers of our friends, our relatives in the love of God, all over the world."

What an amazing hospital—where everybody talks with love and trust about God, where nurses, when they are not busy, pray for their patients and read meditations and the Bible at night. In this hospital, where I came back on Sunday evening, I found them all praying and singing in a side room, gathered around a very ill old lady who had just been brought in. It might not be considered the most efficient care in an ICU, but they trusted their God to take care of my husband and the two premature babies while they were on another assignment of love.

This so-called 'underdeveloped' continent has a living faith and a HEART. One may wonder which part of the world is really underdeveloped.

It is my conviction that the healing of the world ultimately lies in Africa, whatever the appearances to the contrary. One day, when along with the rest of the world, they have finished their fighting, and brought their spirituality in balance with their materialism, it will become manifest that here the heart of the world has been kept intact. In this crisis we were supported by the brother-sisterhood in Jesus, in Allah, in the Lord Shiva, in Sai Baba, and in the God of the 'unbelievers'. This brother-sisterhood is what the Africans all over the continent find in God, and which, one day, will prevail and come to bloom.

There was no department of cardiology in any hospital in Gabarone and so, three days later, when his heart had stabilized, Pieter was airlifted to Johannesburg. In South Africa, cardiology is of the highest standard in the world; after all, the very first heart transplant ever performed was done there.

Our insurance company had organized everything for us and, accompanied by a doctor and nurse, the three of us traveled in a luxurious, specially equipped business jet. Costyn was over the moon. This was a dream come true for him, arranged by divine love after he had instantly dropped everything to come over. Even Pieter was well enough to enjoy the treat.

God is perfection, so there was a special office in the hospital that arranges accommodation for the relatives of patients who come from abroad. They found us a bed-and-breakfast with devoted Christians, who took care of us with the most gentle love and understanding. Every evening the family prayed for the patients and their relatives and for the medical staff that takes care of them.

This afternoon we came back to Gabarone.

Baba's miracle of love—I have him back. During those first dreadful twenty-four hours, I never imagined that this could ever happen. Whenever I came home to call, I had looked around the house so sadly, thinking how I would have to dismantle it soon. In my mind I was selling the lovely new furniture again, and the curtains, and the car, and packing up the few things I wanted to keep.

He is back in our sweet little house, instead—weak, but confident that all will be well. At times my heart seems to overflow with gratitude.

I have received him back unimpaired, and I know that he will live happy and fulfilled for the remainder of his days, doing the work he loves, as was my pact with God.

He does not remember anything—not even the initial pain—from the moment he told me to call the nurse until he came to. This afternoon, though, he told me that he heard me talk to him and he heard me pray. We all thought he was unconscious, but he heard me. I was so moved.

Sai Baba says that if we die with the name of God on our lips, by whatever name he is near and dear to us, we have forever finished with the earth. It is the sign that there is nothing more to learn here, and we will not come back unless we so wish. I have often thought of how I was praying the Gayatri Mantra for him with my hand on his heart. I love to believe that he would have gone straight to God, on the sound of this most holy prayer.

I surrendered him to the Father. My only demand had been that he would be well to express his being on earth, if he would stay.

I accepted that the time might have come for his soul to go, and I did not want to hold him back. I conveyed this to him and he heard.

My own faith and the support of all the prayers, near and far, gave me the courage to release him. This was my ultimate declaration of love for him and for our Creator. Carried by all, his love for us and for the earth and for life itself brought him back. We are so thankful.

The support of our son was invaluable. Tomorrow he will travel back and take up his normal life again. God gave him a big lesson in service when he literally dropped everything from his hand to come. While we had to wait for the heart treatment, it was often quite boring in Johannesburg, but he was patient and understanding. The event had shaken me to the core, and he was there to listen and help me through grief and shock.

Pieter had not wanted to die. His great love for Africa and his dedication to the people—expressed in his work to provide them with water, the basic need of life—came back to him when he was the one who needed the water of life. In his struggle to survive, he basked in the faith and the warmth of the African people who took care of him. In a time span of two hours, four times Africa got his heart beating again and has kept it beating up till today.

To me the Father is the Source, the Infinite, the Nameless and the Formless, but also the intensely Personal. Loving and caring, he expresses himself in and through all who are willing to be his Mind, his helping hands, his comforting words, and His brilliant medical science. The formless takes form in whatever love needs to manifest itself.

Your will be done, for ever and ever,
Amen,
Sai Ram.

Constance, Pieter and Costyn

The Streets of Nairobi

Holy Other: You are my past, my present, my now
and my eternity. (A Course in Miracles)

Over fifty thousand children live in the streets of Nairobi.
Some of them have run away from home because of their parent's
violent behavior. Child abuse is a great problem in the country.
Many children have been thrown out of the house when the
umpteenth child was born to their slum mother, who could no
longer feed the rest of her brood. Others can still come home, but
are sent out to beg during the daytime. With Aids quietly working
its way to a pinnacle, more and more are orphans who have
nowhere to go but in the streets. By day, and even more so at
night, the children are fleeing the police and other ruthless people
who are out to crush, exploit and rape them.*

And in all their misery they can be so adorable. A small
crowd of them was always roaming around the shops where I used
to go. In the daytime they gathered on the big traffic circle nearby
from where they had a good overview over the surrounding area of
the roads, the shops and their customers, and the police.

One day a dirty little boy of about ten years old came to
greet me, and said with a slight reproach in his voice,

"Eh, Mama, there you are. Where have you been so long?"

"I have been abroad for some time," I justified myself.

"You promised me gumboots," he exclaimed, unmistakably
indignant this time.

I didn't think I had ever seen him before.

"Ehum... did I?"

"Yes, remember" he ordered, "last month."

I hesitated. "It must have been someone else, I think."

I looked into his eyes. They were laughing and a bit
anxious at the same time. After all, he had to get me to the shoe
shop.

"No", he said firmly, "it was you."

He clearly did not understand how I could be so dumb as
to have forgotten, and he began to lose patience with me.

---

* The new government is making a serious effort to combat
corruption and improve the fate of street children.

"You know, Mama, the rains have come and my feet get very cold in the evening. We go buy them now," and he pulled at my hand. I laughed. He was so naughty and so charming.

"Please Mama?" he pleaded.

I gave in. An earnest discussion followed on the price of a pair of gumboots, because the question now was if I had enough money with me. He knew exactly how much they cost—which should have made me suspicious—and it was considerably more than the packet of milk or the bunch of bananas I usually gave the children.

I knew I was not being reasonable. There were regular, well organized ways of getting clothing to the street children and I should follow those. But then, I was delighted, and God did not promise us a reasonable paradise, did he? The child's pluck and charm made me glow, and my little friend was going to have warm feet when the streets were cold.

He decided that we should go to the shoe shop in the luxurious shopping mall two streets further down. I suggested that we should walk there, but of course he didn't want to hear of it.

"We take the car. You can park it there, very safe with the guards. That's better. Come on, let's go!"

We walked over to the car; he was skipping with joy and my heart danced. I unlocked the door and he climbed in the front seat with a blasé face as if he never traveled any other way, but I could see that, underneath, he enjoyed himself hugely. During the short drive—his head reaching just above the dashboard—his main activity was to look out of the windows and see if any of his comrades were around to observe his glory.

We entered the gate of the shopping mall and I parked the car. And then, when he got out, he had his supreme moment of glory. With his nose disdainfully up in the air, he looked right through the guard who always chased him and his friends away.

His shabby clothes did not seem to bother him in the least among all the well-dressed rich, and cheerfully chatting we walked through the mall. The shoe shop was on the first floor. Eagerly he dashed in. It took him about ten minutes to check out every single shoe on display and its price, and only then was he ready to sit down.

"My friend here needs gumboots," I declared to the girl who came to help us. She looked as if she was smelling something rather bad, but what could she do but measure his dirty foot and go and get a few samples? The child had no problem making up his mind. A nice, strong pair he chose and his eyes were as shiny as the new boots.

When I paid at the counter, I worried, "Won't the bigger boys rob him of his boots?"

"He will not lose them to others, not that one," the lady assured me with a knowing smile and a sidelong glance at the boy. She was clearly cleverer than I. But then, I was not being clever, was I? I was busy being happy.

"Where are you going to keep them?" I asked him.

"In my grandmother's house," he answered. I felt relieved. At least there was someone in his life he belonged to. "And I'll put them on when I go to church on Sunday."

When everything was settled, I dropped him off where I had found him.

"Don't you put them on now?" I asked when we said goodbye.

"No, not yet, I'll take them home in the evening."

"But where will you keep them until then?" I wondered where a street kid could keep anything safe from preying colleagues.

"Don't you worry, Mama, I know where to hide them." And on that we parted.

I saw him often in the years to come, but I never ever saw the boots again. Whenever I asked him about them, he always told me stories, and in the end I did not bother anymore. He had clearly sold them straightaway.

I watched him grow up. One of the shopkeepers told me that he ran away from every child's home where charitable people and welfare organizations tried to place him. A structured life had become too much of a prison to him.

These children often sniff glue. They have a small plastic bottle filled with strong shoemakers glue and they breathe in the fumes through their nostrils. The more hardened ones have a bottle hanging permanently in their nose. The poisonous fumes of the glue affect the brain to dull the hunger pains, but gradually they also severely damage it.

The boy's eyes became duller, and at times even had a slightly mad expression. I could not make contact with him any more. It was sad, but there was nothing I could do about it. That one happy afternoon we had together, however, we carry as a shining little treasure hidden in our souls. Shoemaker's glue, hunger, nor madness can affect the soul, and the love and the joy we shared hold us connected forever.

Life in Nairobi, in Africa, is a constant challenge to find a way of dealing within oneself with the despair of others. Even to go shopping for the daily necessities is a direct confrontation with streets kids, hawkers, and refugees queuing in front of the gates of United Nations High Commission for Refugees.

Drought and hunger bring millions to the capital in the hope of finding work. Most of them end up in abject slums, and the streets are full of desperate hawkers, beggars, street children and, unfortunately, thugs.

The street hawkers in the capital have a miserable and dangerous existence.

I often bought flowers from one of the flower sellers in the shopping area near us.

Flowers are an important export product for Kenya. Every night a few planeloads full leave for in The Netherlands to be auctioned in Aalsmeer, close to Amsterdam, and from there are sent out into the world. The ones that are not perfect, or miss the plane, are released to the local market, and so there is always an abundance of cheap, beautiful fresh flowers for sale on the streets. The hawkers buy them in bulk from the middlemen and then arrange their wares nicely in buckets on the sidewalk, in the shade of the trees.

"Your price has gone up since last week," I said to the men, admiring their sweet smelling roses, lilies and carnations.

"That's how we have to buy them now," one boy answered.

"How is business these days?" I asked. We started a conversation about his trade and his life, and the others joined in. They told me how little they managed to earn.

"Don't you have a job for me, Mama?" one of them asked. "I am married and I have a baby daughter now. I can't earn enough with the flowers." He was a nice boy with an open face.

"I used to be a gardener, but the people left and I could not find another job," he added despondently. When the contract in Botswana was finished, we had moved back to an apartment in Nairobi, but I promised that I would come back for him if ever we would have a house with a garden again.

In the evening rush hour, they try their luck with the cars in the traffic jam at the traffic circle. Unfortunately, it is an unnerving affair to stop and buy flowers from them there. The men are desperate to come home with some money, so the moment you open your window, five of them push their biggest bunch inside the car. The price they ask is related to the type of car you drive, but it is always outrageous. You try to push a couple of bunches out of your face in an effort to make a bid, but your voice is drowned in the wrangling of all of them shouting at the same time how much they will come down 'for you, my special friend'. The street is narrow and you block the passage for the cars behind you, and their drivers begin to honk furiously.

You either try to escape because you cannot handle the chaos, or you quickly settle with one. This only makes matters worse. As you slowly pull up the car, and at the same time try to roll up your window in the hope that the rest will withdraw their flowers, they push their bunches even more in your face. Running alongside the car they implore, "Please, take mine too? I'll give you a special price," and they come down at every two meters you advance in your car.

"It is very dangerous work," my guy told me, "especially after dark."

On the equator, throughout the year it gets dark between quarter to seven and quarter past seven when rush hour begins to subside somewhat.

"Many drivers accelerate on purpose and you have to jump not to get hit. They don't care about you," my guy told me.

The others joined in angrily, "A car hit our friend here and his leg was broken. They try to hit you for sport, especially after dark."

Their worst enemy is the police. Those lovelies keep a close eye on the boys, and when they see that they have earned some money, they 'arrest' them. They rob them of their earnings, take them to the station and keep them locked up in a cell during the night. The next day the boys are taken to a court, where corrupt judges who don't care, fine them money they don't have. If they are lucky, their relatives manage to locate them quickly, and as soon as they can come up with the needed amount, the men are released from prison—however, not before having paid money for 'lunch' to the police as well. They go back to their sidewalk to find their delicate wares spoiled, of course, or stolen, and they have to buy a fresh supply. Inevitably there always comes a time when they can no longer find the money to restock. Then they join the ranks of the desperate destitute, or worse, the criminals.

Nairobi in a nutshell.

Africa is a continent where millions of people are fleeing one another. They flee from country to country, from region to region, from town to town, within the town from one area to another, and from street to street.

The images are all too familiar. On the TV screen, endless masses of frightened people parade before our eyes. They are on the way. They hold their children by the hand and carry their meager possessions on their heads. Others 'have arrived'. Woefully they sit in wretched camps and gradually restructure their lives within those limitations—or not. Their lives are broken, their bodies dilapidated, and their minds dulled with hopelessness.

The pain in our heart makes us wonder if we are looking at the manifestation of our own hunger. Emaciated, with despair in their eyes, might these fellow humans be the extreme manifestation of our own craving for more? Do they mirror back to us our own belief in lack of love? And what are we fleeing?

Apart from street children and the jobless poor without legal rights, Kenya has had a cross section of the different kinds of refugees Mother Earth is carrying. High up in the dry and infertile North, in the nineties, there were camps with Ethiopians, Sudanese and Somalis who had fled the civil wars in their countries.

There were even camps for displaced Kenyans, some of which dated from as far back as 1992, the year when the government had given way to the pressure of the donor community to allow a multi-party system. These refugees were people who had migrated from their area of origin to make a living in other parts of the country, a normal procedure in most of the world. But if they were from a tribe that supported the opposition, they were chased away by force if they happened to live in an area where the government needed to win. The ensuing violence had been branded 'tribal clashes', but many considered it to be political terrorism, instigated by the ruling government party.

Those people had given up their life in the region they originated from, and they had nowhere to return to and no means to start afresh. Eventually they were gathered in camps, where they did not receive food aid or medical care, and died a slow death. Many are still displaced even now.

The bureaucracy of the UN organization for refugees, situated close to the traffic circle with the street children and the hawkers, is so complicated that even the most urgent cases take a long time to deal with. Day in, day out, long queues wait in front of the gate for things that do not happen, coming back the next day to the same.

To look stark naked destitution in its living face is a shock to the heart, the mind, and all we take for granted in life. The help we may give is never enough and continuously we revolt against our limitations. What can we do after we have donated money, clothes and some food? We can switch off the TV, but we cannot switch off their suffering, and the pain in us stays. We are watching our own failure. What in the name of God do we have in common with them? We have recognized powerlessness and victimization. In the desert of the hunger and thirst of our materialism, we are on the run from the war within ourselves. Maybe we are running the wrong way? Might there be a way towards peace?

Sai Baba says, 'Hands that help are holier then lips that pray,' so whoever has ears to hear and a heart to see, becomes a micro aid-organization.

The easiest thing to do is to provide practical help. Either alone or mobilizing friends, we can organize food, clothing, medical care and, sometimes, jobs. Depending on our personal budget, we finance schooling for children or young adults.

We can also try to activate a support network. As a white person—a Mzungu—we have a rather easy access to the financial resources of the rich world.

When all the practical possibilities have been exhausted, when we can do nothing more to help within the scope of our own life—then comes the best part. Then there is nothing left to give but attention and love.

It becomes an experience of love for both to look the dirty little street girl in the eye as one human being to another, instead of shooing away the nuisance; to put an arm around her meager shoulders and have a little chat and briefly to allow her to be a child.

Who does not crave to be truly seen by others? I know I am. Love is the fulfillment of my being. Not only do I feed a child with bread and milk from the shop, but when I allow her to be a fellow human being instead of a pitiful object, she becomes God's gift to me too. When this filthy little girl lovingly looks up at me with her magnificent soft eyes and says, "God bless you, Mama," for a moment she also stills my hunger with the food of joy and gratitude.

In the grief of my powerlessness to heal her life and my own, my heart had cried, "God help!" And God had answered,

"I have helped, I have sent you to her and her to you. Her blessing for you is mine!"

> Your sweet face
> Engraved into my senses,
> In time and over time
> Becomes a memory.
> Your sweetness joined with mine
> Showed me my heart.

It is love to overcome the revolt against our feeling of powerlessness and quietly sit with a Somali Moslem lady in a multi-religious get-together; to listen with compassion to the story of how her husband and her brother were murdered and how she herself escaped with her children and her old father. Once a lecturer at the University of Mogadishu, in her endless wait for papers she now lives without legal status as a fugitive in a very poor area of the town, even though there is a dire shortage of educational staff in the University of Nairobi. All day long, she has to watch out for the police with their machine guns, not interested in arresting her, but in grabbing whatever little money she might have.

We, on the run from our unhappiness, may not be as different from the refugees of life as we think. If we allow their compelling plight to induce our search for ourselves, they may become a mirror and our teachers by reflecting back to us what we lack. And after we have traveled the whole scale of emotions of pity, guilt, grief and anger, finally our powerlessness sends up sighs of despair from the heart, and Spirit in us begins to pray.

Praying is going home, to the peace of the paradise we think we lost. In prayer our emotions become Spirit. A moment long, we forgive ourselves our powerlessness and the world its cruelty. Grief and guilt grow into a compassion, which embraces others in that warm flow of love from the heart that brought Krishna, Buddha and Jesus to earth—who came for the love of us, refugees from paradise.

Jesus said, "My Father's mansion has many dwellings." Could he not also have meant that these dwellings are the human hearts, in which is hidden the peace that 'passeth all understanding'?

We, too, are craving for a home and long to build a dwelling place within ourselves. We, too, often have to go through all the phases of homelessness, losing health, money, job, home, faith and, at times, even our loved ones. We may lose faith in love, but the one thing we can never lose is love itself. It is always with us. It is within us. It is the healing of life on earth. It is the way back to paradise. Love is who we are.

Father, our name is one with Yours. In it we are united with all the living things and You Who are their one Creator.

(A Course in Miracles)

A Cuckoo on the Equator

The radiance of the light was of an even greater intensity than usual at the shores of Lake Victoria, and the whole of nature seemed to hold its breath. Even the hum of the voices in the neighborhood sounded subdued, as if in anticipation of something unheard of.

I sat on the low wall outside my kitchen door and drank in the resplendent red of the hibiscus flowers and the bursts of bougainvillea-purple against the blue sky. The flowering lemon tree smelled sweeter than ever, the scent of the wild herbs seemed filled with joy, and I sensed expectancy even in the sound of the birds.

It was the fifth of May 2000, and a rare and mysterious event was about to take place. At ten o'clock in the morning, all the planets would be positioned in one line with the earth. A new energy was going to be passed on from the sun as an influx of Mother-Love from our Creator, for us to be used to build a better world for ourselves and all and everything we share the planet with. The most ancient of seers have known of this day, and it was going to herald healing, renewal and empowerment.

The full alignment would last only a few minutes. For me, it happened during daytime and, with the sun high in the sky, I would not be able to see anything. Still, my sign came.

A cuckoo called. I was too awake to think that I was dreaming, but in May there are definitely no European Cuckoo on the equator. They come as migrants during the European winter, but then they do not make themselves heard, as they only sing in nesting time.

I heard it again, this sound, at the same time full and hollow, which fills the sky above the meadows in my home country in spring. And now I began to believe my ears. After all, we had been told to expect miracles this day. I received mine. The cuckoo sounded a third time,

"The animal world brings you a sign of renewal."

On the days prior to the event, I had concentrated on it during my meditation and I had clearly felt that Divine Mother-Love also would uplift the animal kingdom into a higher awareness of self. As a consequence, the animals, supported by the earth and her invisible nature beings, were going to have a greater capacity to heal the relationship with humans; to teach them more respect for all life and to remind them of love and moral values.

Millions of animals—sick and healthy ones alike—had recently been slaughtered in Europe in foot-and-mouth disease and BSC epidemics, a harsh and cruel reflection of the loss of faith in the love of God. Both man and animals had forgotten their reality as co-creatures in God and it had come back to all with a vengeance.

The origin of the contemporary cruel and disrespectful exploitation of animals is greed. Greed is fear. It is the expression of the fear that God does not love us and did not create enough for all. In its abundance of leaves, flowers and fruits, every tree shows us the contrary, but we don't believe it. This deep belief in the lack of God's love makes us suffer in many ways, but the ensuing human abuse of animals also has imprinted the same 'belief' of being powerless victims on their collective consciousness.

In an attempt to rock this belief to the core, the animal world brought a great sacrifice. The horrendous scale of the diseases they manifested and the actual threat it has posed to human health, has forced us to re-think.

May my story of love and pain and its solution, be a gentle monument in their honor.

The Animal World has its very own mind.

From Nairobi, we had come to live in Kisumu, in Western Kenya, for a couple of months. We had been given a nice house in a row of five, and the best thing about it was the magnificent view of Lake Victoria, the greatest lake in Africa.

Even though we now had a garden again, one thing was sure. Never again was I going to have animals. Within two years time, I had suffered the heartbreak of parting with six darling dogs, five cats and four kittens, and our very affectionate parrot. On top of that, I had given away twenty well-fed goldfish in the fishpond with their nine-year old clan-mother Gwendolyn, ten beautiful tropical fish from the tank, eight chickens—each with their own name—and about a million bees.

And so there she was! One sweet morning we found an utterly adorable kitten on our doorstep. She was radiating love and crying for food.

There were ten houses in the compound, most with permanent tenants, but of course she had to choose us. We knew from experience how easily we become attached, and so this time we decided on a hard line of action. We would feed her but we would definitely not allow her inside.

The cat must have laughed. Within two days she was all over the house. She was in the kitchen, pleading with us to open the fridge, sat in the windowsill watching the birds, and slept on our bed as if she never had been away. And of course we were delighted as ever with this little innocent being the animal kingdom had presented us with once more. Once de-wormed and properly fed, she grew up into a lovely healthy animal and we basked in her love as she did in ours. She seemed to be born just to be sweet.

We were not the only ones who found her attractive. While we thought she still was a kitten, too soon she got pregnant. Since we would have to return to the flat in Nairobi where we could not keep animals, this was, of course, just what we needed.

The house was at the shore of the lake. In the pristine early morning light, I loved to read and meditate in the garden with the trees, the flowers, and the sparkling birds around me. In the warm sun and the fragrant breeze, the invisible world was with me too, the spirits of water and wind, of animals and plants, of the raging afternoon storm and its heavy downpours, of the thunder and the spectacular electric storms over the hills at night.

"Come on, Kiddies, let's go paint," I used to invite them upstairs with me to my studio when I was ready for action.

And they did. They loved it.

First I did my share of the work. I applied water, paint and finally the paper on the glass plate. That being done, I then took a few steps away from the table and invited them to come in and take part in the process. When I felt they were done playing with water and color, I pulled off the paper and put it on the floor to dry.

They were as curious as I to see what came out, and while I worked back in the painting to bring them out for the world to see, I sensed them watching, and at times nudging me on.

Then the moment came that Pussycat delivered her four strong, healthy kittens. We kept the nest, warm, earthly, and heavenly at the same time, in the bedroom next to the studio, and from that moment on I had no say over my paintings any longer. I was allowed to provide water, paper, and the colors, but the rest the nature beings could very well take care of themselves, thank you very much.

Whatever I made was taken over. A Phoenix rose up tall, and ready for a new life; a blue and pink mythical horse appeared in full gallop; a herd of heavy elephants, grounded earth beings in black, gray and gold; a yellow and red rooster, ready for battle, birds in flight, and a gracefully diving dolphin in blue. All of them were delightful and as full of life and movement as the kittens.

One of the kittens, a black and white male, was remarkably different from the others. This one had come with a mission. His passion was human beings. Already a few days after birth, he began to lift his head at the sound of a human voice. And as soon as his little paws could somehow carry him, even while he was suckling, he would leave his mummy and toddle out of the nest toward the person coming into the room. Any human, familiar or unknown, was important enough to leave the source of life for and go and greet—inbred African courtesy.

The time came that I had to think of finding them all a good home. I began to do the usual things. I put up notices in shops. I asked around in the neighborhood. I lured people to the house to see my treasures and hopefully have their hearts melt. For all my effort, I found a home for two babies and that was it. No one wanted Mummy and two more kittens.

When I had only two weeks left before we would go back to the capital, I got truly nervous. I asked everyone everywhere. I stopped strangers in the street and in the cars that entered the compound with visitors for the other families. I got so upset. Why didn't anybody respond to my charming smiles and flowering descriptions of the most special cats in the world? I became so anxious that I could not even enjoy them anymore.

Twenty years in Africa had taught me how to deal practically, emotionally, and spiritually with the heart-breaking problem of the street children and the desperately poor, the vulnerable, powerless victims of our society. I had accepted that God expects us to do what we can within the context of our lives, and then surrender them to him, blessing them in the knowledge that He loves them as his own creations.

Over the years, I had learned about animals that they, too, choose their incarnation, and so I could allow them to share in the responsibility for their existence. Still, I never managed to apply these high insights when I saw them suffering. Their vulnerability and their innocent defenseless-ness never ceased to tear my heart apart, and however many stray dogs or cats I picked up from the streets, there were always many more, hungry, uncared for, and unloved. For me, the love of Father-Mother Creator excluded the suffering animals. Whenever I found them or they found their way to me, I felt that they were solely my responsibility. And now I failed my cat and her babies.

At night I imagined my purring darlings in the streets, starving, filthy, thin, sick, full of worms and craving for love. I became so distressed that I could hardly even enjoy my paradise any longer.

I had big, one-sided discussions with the Creator:

"Dear Lord, you gave me these adorable creations of yours; I did not ask for them. I did not even want them. It cannot be your will that they go back to the street now." In turns I pleaded, I begged, I trusted, or I was angry with him.

You will never guess his answer. He sent me another cat! From the wild area next to the house, a crying ginger jumped on my windowsill and landed on the terrace. He was absolutely revolting. He had a wide, wild head. His ribs were sticking through his scraggly fur, his body was full of wounds and his ears were half eaten away by fungus. And he was purring as loud as he could, reaching up to my hands to be stroked.

I was so confused that I burst out laughing. There I was, not even able to take care of a couple of beautiful healthy cats and now I was supposed to take on this filthy sick one as well? But my fridge was full of cat food, so could I let him starve? Of course I fed him.

Time closed in. The kittens grew bigger and more playful by the day, but poor mummy began to sense my distress. And purring ginger was coughing his lungs out.

It was eating me day and night, and I became more and more miserable. My beautiful, sweet pussycats were depending on no one but me, and I could not keep them loved and protected.

In my paradise at night, with the nest at stroking distance of my bed, with the moon shining over the lake, the nightjars crying, and the hippos snorting under my bedroom window, I stayed awake with unhappiness.

"Dear God, I need a home for my cats, NOW! What is it that I have to learn here?" No answer, only more stomach ache.

I printed out big photographs of the sweet lot, stuck them on a cardboard and walked over with it to the Sunday bazaar of a primary school next door. When I came to the gate, a small Indian man just came out. In an impulse, I held up my poster and asked,

"Do you want a cat?"

"Oh yes," he radiated, "I'll take two! I love cats. I will call you tomorrow to let you know when I can come and collect them," and we exchanged phone numbers.

Suddenly a heavy weight dropped off my shoulders. My heart told me that God had provided the answer to my prayers.

Of course he did not call the next day and so my anxiety again increased by the hour. See? I had failed once more, and so had God, for that matter.

Finally I picked up my courage and dialed his number. His wife answered the phone.

"Oh dear, but that is impossible. What was he thinking? I know he loves cats, but we cannot take them, we have two ferocious watch dogs."

Shocked, I poured out my whole story, and immediately she became so sweet. "Of course God does not want them in the streets. Don't you worry; we will help you. Just give me a couple of days," she comforted me.

Within two days she brought me a young African vet who took them all. Mummy and daughter would go to a loving home and stay together. When I suggested the vet to put very ill ginger to sleep, he flatly refused,

"No way, I am going to cure him and find him a home. If I can't find one, I'll keep him myself."

We manifest what we believe. My conviction that God is absent in the suffering of animals had made me perceive him as absent. Ginger represented the animal world, crying for the food of love. My anxiety was mankind's cry for God.

I had found God's answer in the street. My little crowd and I had worked through my pain, and the inner light of another human, the Indian at the school gate, had pulled me over the threshold of fear. Only then could love manifest itself as the solution. The trust of my very special litter, the support of Mother Earth and her beings, and my little Indian friend, had worked a healing for me, and in me, for mankind and the animal world.

We had come home; God loves all as his own

.

From Hell to Heaven in Maseno

The small plane from Nairobi to Kisumu was flying low over the land and below us unfolded the fertile highlands of Kenya. The slopes of the hills were covered with coffee farms, which produce a major export earner for the country. Reflecting the sunlight back to its source, small dams sparkled in the green like diamonds surrounded by emerald.

All of a sudden, the earth dropped steeply down into the Great Rift Valley. This immense crack in the earth begins at the Dead Sea, runs through the Red Sea and cuts deeply through the African continent from Ethiopia, Kenya, and Tanzania up till Malawi. Except for the Maasai who roam around with their cattle, its rocky and virtually barren soil offers nothing for humans to subsist on.

An extinct volcano with a perfectly round crater rose up: the majestic Longonot. And in the far distance the snowy tops of Mount Kenya emerged above its clouds. It stirred memories for Pieter of long and very cold climbs over snow and glaciers, of camping at thirty degrees below zero and getting up at three at night to reach the top in time to witness—from an altitude of 5000 meters—the most glorious sunrise over the vast plains of Africa.

We flew across Lake Naivasha, an oasis in the Rift Valley, a crater lake that provides water for the many commercial flower nurseries, another important export product. With its great variety of both land and water birds, it is also a haven for birdwatchers. Close to the shores, dead trees stand around in the water as remnants from the time the water level was much lower, and their eerie skeletons seem to stick our their arms solely to support the cormorants and the fish eagles.

The lake is only about one and a half hours drive from Nairobi and so the Naivasha Yacht Club has its niche in a bay where it is safe for the members to sail, well protected from the wild winds that often come up by the end of the afternoon. At night, the hippos come out of the water, grumbling and snorting, to graze close to the tents of the campers and to remind them that it is not wise to sail too close to the shores.

The plane climbed up again to leave the valley, and now we were flying over the gentle hills of Western Kenya, an ideal area for growing tea. Only the newly sprouted leaves are picked for export tea and the slopes are covered with a carpet of delicate hues of green and yellow.

We made a stopover at Eldoret International Airport. An ambitious government member, who had succeeded in getting his hands on funds that originally had other destinations, had constructed a three hundred million dollar airport, which was used by only one cargo flight a week. A huge chartered Russian cargo plane stood at the side of the runway as a monstrous incongruity in this sleepy little provincial town.

We had to stay on board while a couple of passengers got off. Two airport ground staff took out some luggage, put it on a trolley, and pushed it towards the arrival hall. When it passed by our window, behind us someone suddenly jumped up and shouted:

"They are taking my suitcases!"

The man dashed out, down the stairs, and ran after the trolley. The subsequent shouting and gesticulating between the passenger and the ground staff was a welcome distraction for the bored travelers inside. We could not hear anything but we could well imagine the excited 'yes' and 'no' and 'which ones?' flying around. The scene ended when they offloaded a couple of suitcases, carried them back into the plane, and the man returned to board again

I had followed the performance with great interest. I was in an outgoing mood, so I had left my chair and stood in the doorway to wait for him and start a conversation. He seemed to be in his sixties. He was wearing a blue baseball cap and a bright yellow jacket, and I couldn't figure him out at all. He was definitely not a tourist, or he would have been decorated with a cluster of cameras on his chest. Was he a flower grower, a farmer, or a visiting consultant?

"You're lucky that you saw them taking away your stuff, aren't you? It might have taken you a while to get it back from this 'International Airport'."

"You can talk Dutch," was the rather blunt answer in that language.

I was taken aback. After all my years of talking English, albeit in African countries, I was so proud that the British no longer asked me,

"You are Dutch, aren't you?" but that I had graduated to:

"Where are you from?"

He said that my unmistakable Dutch intonation had given me away. Most of the people with whom I shared the English language were not British born, and so I had never really made an effort to master the singsong that characterizes the language and is one of its most difficult aspects to learn. Even among the

British, there are so many differences in accent that I never knew whom to imitate. I imitated them all. I spoke Kenyan English with the Kenyans, Indian with the Indians, and if I happened to be with someone real British, like my parrot, I tried my best.

Standing in the open doorway of the plane, he told me that he was a retired surgeon and came to do volunteer work in a poor hospital in a small town near Kisumu. He had taken the night flight from Amsterdam to Nairobi. He had had to wait six hours for this connection, and after arriving in Kisumu he would still have to travel another two hours by car to his final destination. The last thing he needed was trouble with his luggage. Apart from the hassle of trying to make them get their act together and send it on, he would need it straightaway. He was bringing in materials like syringes, medication, surgical tools, and gloves, things that are always in short supply, or absent altogether, in the hospitals for the poor.

The rest of the trip was brief. We descended along the shores of Lake Victoria and, while he circled around to get in the right position to land, the pilot treated us to a beautiful view of the coastline and the town.

Arriving at Kisumu airport is a unique experience. It is a pleasure to walk down the stairs, off the plane, and be caressed by the soft, warm air and the carmine-red flowers of the flamboyant trees that shout their brilliant welcome. You walk out of the gate and you look around for the arrival hall. There isn't any, or rather, it is right there. It is the roadside outside the gate.

Everybody gathers on the street and the narrow sidewalk, and relatives and friends greet each other in a noisy mixture of color and race. Kenyans, in different hues according to their tribes, make their way through light brown Indians, and they all make us Europeans look very white indeed.

One by one, the luggage trolleys come rolling out of the gate and everyone tries to get hold of their bags and suitcases at the same time. Taxi drivers urge passengers for business, grabbing their luggage before they can refuse, and private drivers push their big, four-wheel drives through the crowd to pick up their Important Person.

It is a splendid arrival hall with the whole of the blue sky as a roof. I have never had the pleasure of arriving in the pouring rains that come down quite often in the late afternoon, but it seems that Kenya Airways does provide a couple of umbrellas!

There was a small committee from the hospital to welcome our new doctor friend. We had found a taxi and we said goodbye to him and we repeated our invitation to come and see us whenever he would be in Kisumu-town.

The Dutch organization that sponsored his visit had also given him an amount of money to buy some basic hospital supplies locally, like bandage material, soap, and disinfectants, and so he came to town about ten days later. After he had finished his shopping, he visited us and he told us how he had found a standard Kenyan up-country hospital.

"It consists of simple wooden barracks in dire need of paint and just about everything else," he said. Occasionally we had visited such hospitals, so we could picture what he was talking about.

"The medical and maintenance staff receive a miserable salary," he continued. "Right now, they haven't had any payment for three months. I don't understand how they survive with their families."

"Aren't they leaving to find other work then?" I asked.

"They can't run away, of course, because they keep hoping that they may still get paid one of these days. It is not amazing that they lose their motivation. And it is nearly impossible to get proper doctors to work for the little money they get—if any at all. Doctors prefer to try their luck in the big cities anyway, for more money and prestige."

This was the second time that he had come to work in this particular hospital, so he had known what to expect and he took it all in his stride.

"You know, they should be able to run this hospital well with the money they earn and the donations they receive from abroad. It is always the same story; mismanagement and corruption make it all mysteriously disappear as fast or as slow as it comes in. And the same happens with the medical supplies, especially the medicines."

This was a known fact. It happened in the hospitals in the big cities, too. Hospital personnel, down to the cleaners, steal the medicines and then sell them in the streets and marketplaces of the villages in the area. Little bags with an attractive, multicolored collection of pills have killed—only God knows how many— gullible, ignorant and desperate people all over Africa.

Our doctor had hoped for a little rest after his long trip, but as soon as he had set foot over the threshold, the staff had begged him to come to the rescue of a woman who had been in labor for three days. The baby was stuck and no one had been able to perform a caesarean to deliver it.

"I quickly put my luggage in my room; I washed my hands and I operated immediately. I managed to save the mother, but the baby was dead. The poor woman is in a terrible state and she definitely won't be able to have any children, after this."

We talked a while about the sorry state of the healthcare for the poor in these countries, and our conversation strayed to the traditional ways of healing. People still visit witch doctors, who perform their ancient rites to ban the bad spirits, which have caused a particular illness. And, of course, they seek help from the herbalists who, for thousands of years, have cured the sick with the plant life that is available in the surrounding countryside.

Then, in the peace of our little paradise at the lakeside, I told him about my gift of facilitating healing in others, with the divine love that lives in us as Spirit.

"I approach illness from a different perspective," I said. "I have learned to see physical illness as much as a cry for healing from the heart as emotional disharmony."

"Physical illness a cry from the heart? What an astonishing idea!" he exclaimed.

"Yes, the expression of an often desperate, unconscious fear to love, but also the fear to be vulnerable and allow yourself to be loved. A cry for love which, in the time of my back operation, even brought me to the point that I had to ask a nurse to pick up a pencil I had dropped on the floor."

"But what does a physical problem have to do with these emotions?"

"You know how people say, 'I'm worried sick.'"

"Yes," he said, "that expresses some of it."

"There is more than worry when life does not develop according to our deepest desire. When we live in anxiety, in permanent stress, when the workload is constantly too heavy, the boss is awful, the competition is stifling, and I don't want to do this work anyway, because it is not who I feel I am. Still, I don't step out, because I cannot drop the burden of financial commitments and the people I am responsible for. You know what I am talking about."

"Or a marriage that has become unbearable because the love and the meaning have gone out of it," he added. "All conditions for stomach ulcers and heart problems."

"The real issue here is, that to leave such a situation means taking a risk. And this asks for courage and trust. Where do you find those if you do not love yourself and do not really believe that others love you enough to take the risks with you?"

"This is how you come to fear as the essence?"

"Fear takes us away from the harmony of body, mind, and heart that is health. We call it stress and the next stage is illness."

"Of course," he said.

"And also, you know the anguish that comes with a severe illness and with pain," I continued, "and the grief, and at times the anger, 'why me, why now?' In this disharmony, we can hardly feel further removed from love, can we?"

"In that case, the physical problem is the cause of the emotional one, not the other way round," he stated.

"But you see how closely they are related," I continued, "so maybe it is possible to solve the problem from either side."

He looked puzzled.

"You tackle physical conflict with your medical science. When you succeed, the harmony of the body is restored and the direct fear is gone."

"The fear to love and be loved?" he asked.

"Hopefully," I answered. "I can help to heal this emotional pain. I work for the heart, from the heart. When I lay my hands on someone who is suffering either physically or emotionally, I connect with the infinite Love, our Source, which is present in and all around us. There is love in everyone, even though their whole lives people may manifest the contrary. I connect with that love and this soothes the patient to the extent that the pain may disappear. When fear makes room for peace and the inner harmony is restored, health can, and often does return."

This was new to our friend but he had listened carefully.

"Then maybe you can help me with this woman I operated on that first evening. I don't know what more I can do to relieve her suffering," was his response. I promised I would reach out to her divine inner being and support her with prayer. On this, he left and went back to the hospital.

During the course of the week he called to invite us to come and visit him in the hospital on Sunday. I asked him how the woman was doing.

"Badly," he answered, "she now has malaria as well, and the wound has become infected."

"Poor woman, how awful. She must be in so much pain."

"Of course I am doing as much as I can, but you know how restricted my resources are here. As a matter of fact, I am trying to get her to a better hospital."

I felt for him and I wondered how powerless he must feel, at times. He knew all the possibilities of the rich world and here he often had access to less than the bare minimum to help these poor Africans.

Then he added, "When I came back from Kisumu at the end of the afternoon, I found her lying on the floor next to her bed, drip and all. She had fallen out of her bed."

"What?"

"When I asked the nurses why they had not put her back in her bed, they said it was not worth the trouble. She would fall out again."

I was speechless, too shocked for words.

"So now she has pneumonia as well."

I was appalled at the indifference of these creatures that had made it their profession to take care of the sick. Without lifting a finger, they had left this woman lying on the cold, hard floor, in great pain from an infected caesarean wound and with high fever from malaria. I could not believe the cruelty of these nurses, women who probably all had borne children themselves. What a difference with our experience in Gaborone!

Sunday came, and we drove to the village. The hospital was high in the hills. This made the place considerably cooler than Kisumu-town, and I thought how much easier this must be on the patients than enduring the heat of the lower areas. The buildings were surrounded by magnificent trees, well-cut grass, and flowerbeds with an abundance of all the lovely flowers that grow so easily in this gentle climate with lots of rain. We had seen worse.

We found our friend in the simple bungalow that he shared with three other guest doctors. There was a young couple from Austria and a lady pediatrician from England, all on a temporary assignment like he was.

He told us his daily routine and he asked us many questions about our life, in an effort to understand what made us stay in Africa for so long. He discussed the perpetual water problems of the hospital with Pieter and we went to see the water storage tanks and the pump system. We walked around the extensive compound. It was so large that part of the land was used for growing vegetables and we wondered whether they were given to the patients or sold on the local market to make up for the lack of salaries.

He took us inside the hospital and opened the operation theatre. To every first-world doctor this room would have been a nightmare, with nothing bright and shiny and a minimum of sterility, but he had what he needed, and it was clean—at least when he was there.

A soft drizzle began to fall. It made the soil itself smell sweet and it seemed to urge me on.

"I would really like to go and sit with the woman now, if you don't mind," I said.

He looked at me with doubt in his eyes.

"Are you sure? She suffers so badly that it has affected her mind, and she is not exactly a sight to make you happy."

"I know, and I don't mind," I said.

"All right then," he agreed, and over a maze of garden paths, he took me to a barrack that stood a little apart from the others. We came to a ward with some ten beds. Six of them were empty, and in three others young mothers were sleeping or nursing their newborn babies.

There she was, in the far corner. The nurses had not even bothered to spare her the heartbreak of being in the same ward with happy mothers and healthy babies, while all she had was a dead baby and a ravaged body.

Our friend took me over to her, and with a few words he introduced me to her sister, who was sitting on the empty bed next to her. Then he left us and I was alone with the two women and God.

Her bed was shabby. At least she had sheets but there was only a cheap hard blanket to cover her. She could neither eat nor drink, and even though she was on the drip, she looked very dehydrated. A wretched bundle of shrunken misery, a cry of shame on humankind seemed to disappear in the hollow of her mattress.

She was restless. With her eyes half closed she was moaning softly, but at times she cried out in a loud, anguished scream. She must have been in so much pain. She was hot with fever and her lips were dry and caked.

I gently wiped her face and her mouth and I stroked her hair. She was a simple woman from the countryside and I doubt she would have understood English even if she had not been half unconscious, but the heart has a language independent of the tongue. I laid my hands on her, and quietly I talked to her about God and his love. I knew her soul would hear me even if she did not. And as my love and my peace flowed into her as a warm, soothing energy, her moaning gradually subsided. At last it stopped altogether.

I sensed angels surrounding us while I talked softly about God, the Ground of our being in whom we are one, and about the love of Jesus, who carries us in his arms. He was so close...

My one hand rested on her shoulder and with the other one I held hers. Slowly, I began to lose the sense of my hands and they seemed to dissolve until they were like clouds of warm energy. My whole body tingled. It became warmer and lighter, and it was as if my skin did not confine me anymore. I expanded into a limitless energy of love and warmth as our Jesus merged with me and filled the room.

Suddenly the silence was broken by a soft sound. I thought she was moaning in pain again, but she was not.

Radiating heat with fever, and with a voice that croaked because of the dehydration and the respiratory infections, she was singing, at first hardly audible, but then louder,

"Thank you, Jesus."

She sang words in her own language that I did not understand, but a few English words kept coming back as a refrain,

"Thank you, Mungu (God). Thank you, Jesus."

In all her unbearable pain of body and heart, she sang for him. This poor creature, rejected by most of her fellow humans, by the earth, and by life itself, in her utter dejection was lifted outside herself as she overcame it all and praised and thanked her Creator whom she must have loved since the beginning of time.

I held her, with tears streaming over my face. Her sister was crying next to me and for a long time we sat without saying anything. The last word had been spoken. I knew she was now free to go.

When I finally got up to leave, I heard her mumble some words. Her sister said, "She says that she wants to come with you."

"Later," I told her, stroking her arm. "You get better first."

As I walked out, I still felt expanded in a cloud of warm love-energy. I knew it was going out to touch all the other patients in the hospital and, hopefully, the nurses as well. And as I walked past the other wards, I felt blessed to be God's instrument, his expression of love and healing.

The next day my heart stayed connected with her, and incessantly it declared to the Creator, "I, divine Love, claim the healing of this child of yours, Father."

The next day our doctor friend called me.

"She died last night, she is gone."

A sudden profound joy opened up in me and made me exclaim, "Oh, that is so beautiful, thank you God!"

A surprised sound came from the other end of the line, but I was too moved to say anything but,

"That is so wonderful!"

"But I tried so hard to save her," he objected sadly.

"To save her for what kind of a life?" I asked passionately. "She could not get any more children, so her husband would probably have thrown her out for another woman. Save her for a life of rejection, poverty, hunger, and grief? Did you test her for HIV?"

In this part of Kenya, Aids is the worst in the whole country, so she was probably infected.

"No, there was no direct reason," he said, "and with the limited material we have here, I can only do the test if there is a clear indication."

"Then she might have lived to develop full blown Aids and start the suffering of dying all over again, while she was so close to going now," I said.

"I did my best to keep the woman alive," he said unhappily.

"But you did," I exclaimed, filled with awe for the power of love, the great chess Master, who had moved us all around to be together at the right time in the right place.

"You kept her alive until you could bring us together and God's love could perform this healing of her soul. Of course she died in dreadful physical misery, but you were there to alleviate it as much as you could. She did not die completely deserted because you cared for her where the staff did not. And she lived long enough to lift her heart and soul above it all, carried by my prayers and her sister's. She died praising her beloved Jesus."

A few days later I was sitting on the terrace of the house, looking at the light playing on the water. As the breeze carried a scent of orange bloom, a cloud of gentle love seemed to touch me. With a certainty that cannot be explained in words, I knew it was she. She came to thank me for the love and the help we had given her, and her being, now at peace, embraced me. She had asked to be with me, and as I live in both worlds, in Spirit as well as on earth, she had come with me as she had wished.

I keep pondering about the mysterious connections of our souls. An unknown woman from deep in the heart of Africa had stayed alive for this doctor from a far country in the North to come and save her. To save her until he could take me to her, and she and I and her sister could take each other to Jesus, who lifted all of us into the love that is the Father.

Someone, who would have died as a reject of life, had passed on instead glorifying the Father—as the Father was now glorifying her. Dying, she had moved into the high being that is her divine reality. Her life had been healed and her death had become a cosmic event of love.

And all this had happened because I had felt like chatting with this man with a blue baseball cap and a bright yellow jacket.

Little had I known, then, that the Heart of Creation was calling us.

Finale

I have played my score for you of how God walks the earth with us, deep within our hearts where we know love.

It sang of recreating paradise from thought to thought and from instant to instant, any time of the day or the night.

All we need, we have. The ears to hear, the eyes to see, a mind to think and a heart to love. With space and time our playground, we have been given a planet full of playmates. We merely have to choose for peace. And once we make up our mind for a change of heart, we set new harmonies in motion. Our mind will grow, our heart will flow, and our eyes will open wide in delight.

Limitations become an invitation to join with others, and obstacles, challenges to harmony. Our space we transform into a haven of peace even if it is a concrete flat in a busy town. Time becomes something to give instead of grab, and six billion people on this planet turn into colleagues and fellow travelers instead of strangers, or worse. When we change our mind to become the instrument of our heart instead of its ruler, we are in tune with the symphony of paradise.

It is not easy. A moment long, our good impulse uplifts us, but then we slide back again into what always was. Our surroundings do not support us, yet, but each time we follow our inspiration and make a choice of wholeness, we venture a step further in the clear stream of the melodies. And, note by note, we reconstruct our symphony, andante, allegro, rondo, and largo.

> Our song is singing about
> To be what we are
> And to do what we do.
> At the moment it is loving you
> And writing to you.
> Then get on with dressing,
> Then clean the room,
> Then have a bite to eat.
> And every moment of even our
> Most insignificant actions
> Is of supreme importance.
> What a relief!
> It leaves
> All the room in the world
> To do something else.

The split second in which we surrender to the silent voice of the heart is our path to peace. It asks for courage. Often we have to go against what we think is right, what others expect from us, or what fits into the rules of society. We will be odd, late, impolite, and unproductive in the eye of the world, but each time we listen to an impulse from our heart, we get a glimpse of our divine potential.

Let us roll up the snake of reason, put it in the wide-open basket of our heart and make it our friend. God created it and saw that it was good. It took on the role of tempter in our mind but it is yearning to be released. When we play the flute, the snake will unfold and dance for us, and it will sway gently to the music of our heart and join the grand finale.

About the Author

Constance van Dongen Eykman tries to find the best and brightest in all that is around her, as she feels that a positive attitude contributes to an energy of hope and joy in the world.

She lived in Holland for many years and then made her home in Africa, in Kenya, Ghana, and Botswana. She traveled in many other countries, like South Africa, Tanzania, Zanzibar, Swaziland, and Uganda.

Constance did not live in Africa merely as a European outsider. She allowed herself to become involved in the lives, minds, and hearts of the African people, and so she was able to discover aspects of the African life that are very different from the ones that are generally known. As a result, she has come to believe that Africa, long known as the 'Dark Continent' is very much a 'Continent of Light' as well, much more than people in the 'West' can ever imagine. Africa, the Cradle of mankind, is indeed the cradle of a great and mighty race.

From her diverse experiences among the African people she lived with, she came to realize that Africa, as much as it is a physical place, is a "State of Mind' as well.

Her experiences in life and travels precipitated the collection of stories found in this volume, "Paradise, A Heartbeat Away -- A spiritual safari in Africa".

But had Constance only been a writer, that would have robbed the world of the other parts of herself that glow as brightly as her ability to chronicle her unique adventures. She is also a fine artist with glorious paintings to her credit. Once a classical singer, the peace and power of her inner world of music translate themselves in her paintings and in the melody and rhythm of her writer's language.

In harmony with the local climate of the places where she lived, with passion she designed lovely colorful gardens, home to sparkling birds, and a source of inspiration for her paintings.

Constance's healing abilities and spiritual wisdom - woven into her stories - have helped many and brought hope and joy into the hearts of countless people.

With her husband Pieter and her son Costyn, she lives in homes in Africa and Europe and she keeps traveling to other exotic and spiritual places like India.

Constance van Dongen Eykman hopes to keep writing, painting, and singing her song for all the world. Pieter works in

Africa assisting various governments and the United Nations with their water projects. Costyn, a wonderful young man, delights in jumping out of airplanes (skydiving) as well as pursuing his artistic and technical career.

http://www.paradiseaheartbeataway.com

Printed in the United States
36272LVS00002B/7-45